# THE COMPLETE GUIDE TO FRACTIONS

## ADDITION, SUBTRACTION, MULTIPLICATION AND DIVISION

### Children's Fraction Books

# Let's learn fraction!

# What is Fraction?

A fraction is a part of a whole. It has a numerator and a denominator.

$$\frac{1}{2} \quad \substack{\leftarrow \text{Numerator} \\ \leftarrow \text{Denominator}}$$

Another way of writing a fraction:

Numerator → $1/2$ ← Denominator

This is an example of a fraction in visual form.
Let us assume that these are just pies.

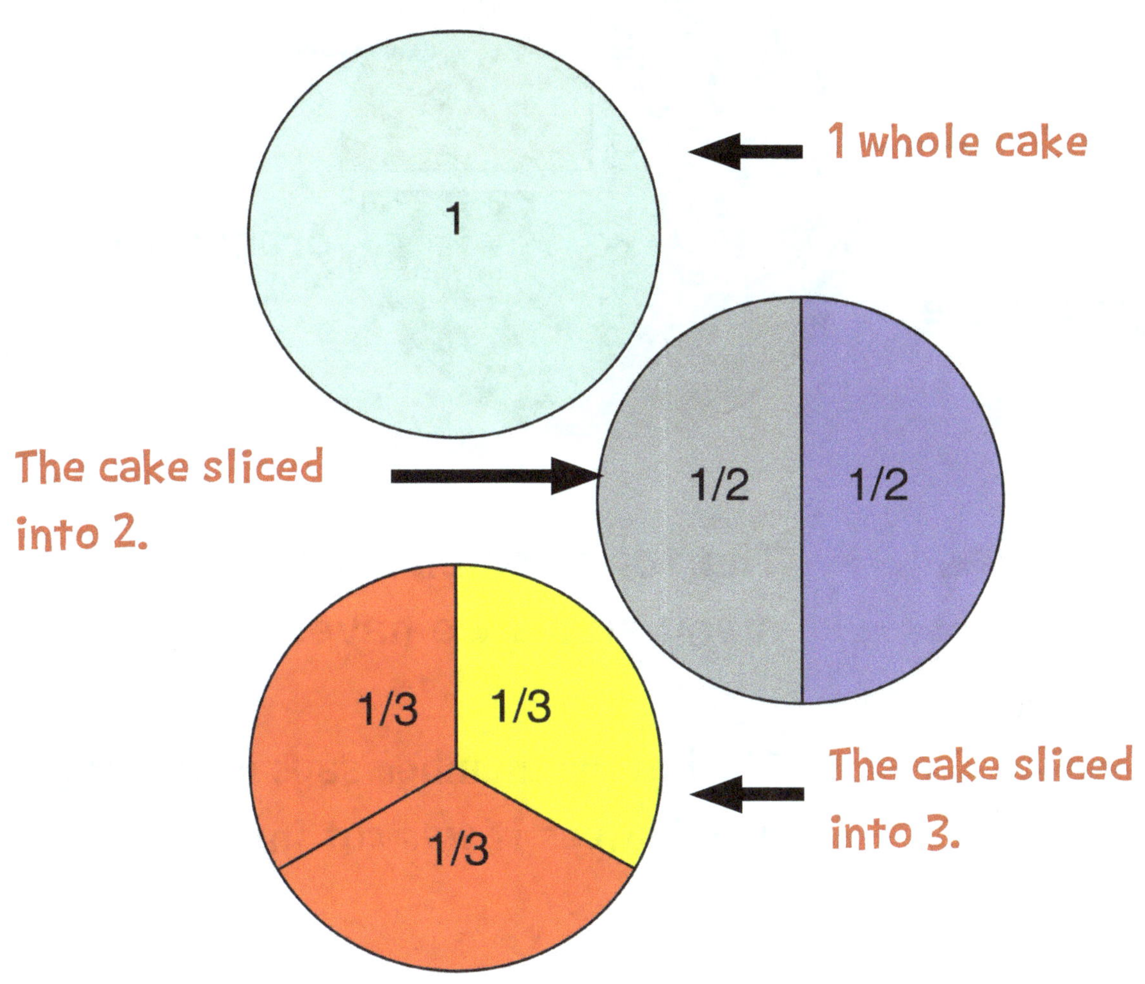

# SAMPLE FRACTIONS

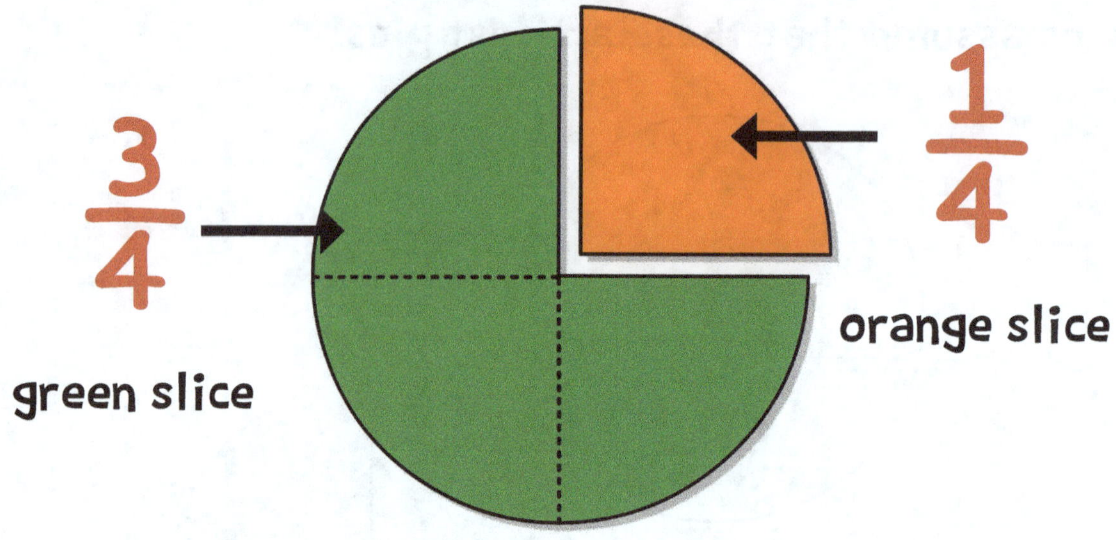


3
4

The top number says how many slices we have.

The bottom number says how many equal slices it was cut into.

# ADDITION OF FRACTIONS
## Visual

**SHADE IN THE FRACTION TO SOLVE THE PROBLEM.**

Ex)

answer: $\dfrac{3}{7} + \dfrac{2}{7} = \dfrac{5}{7}$

## SHADE IN THE FRACTION TO SOLVE THE PROBLEM.

1) 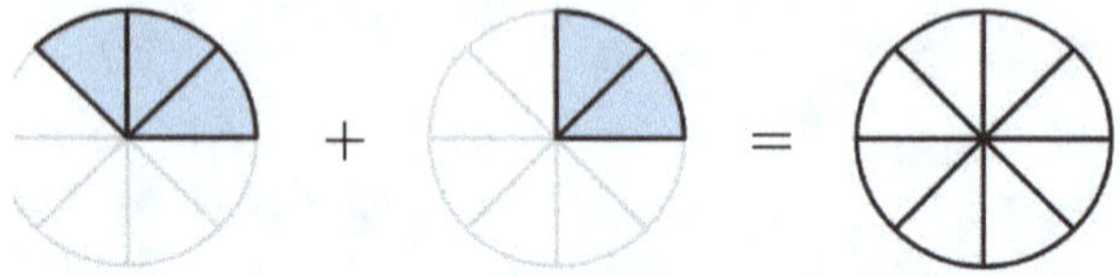     +    =

2) 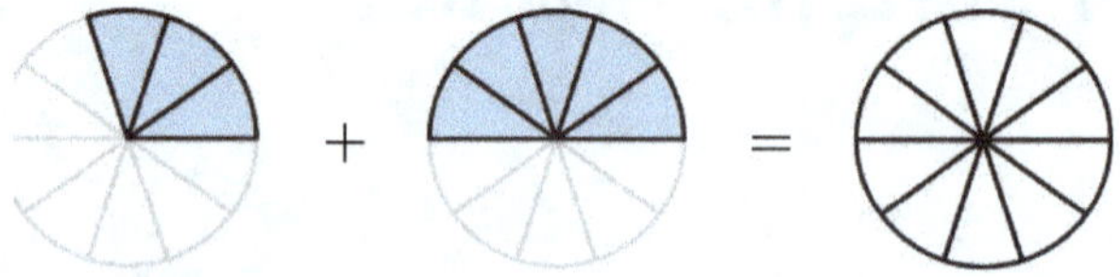     +    =

3) 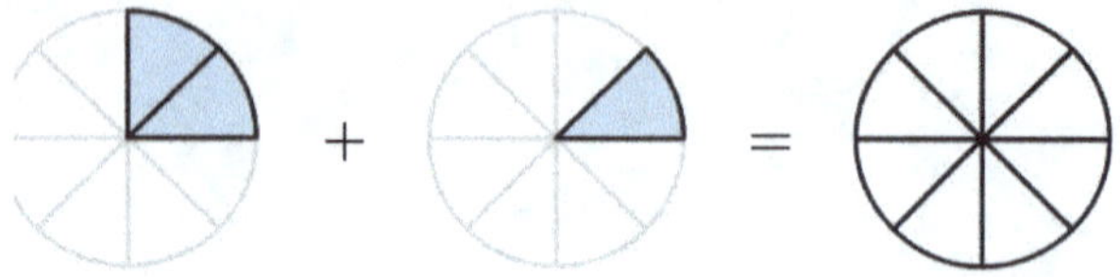     +    =

4) 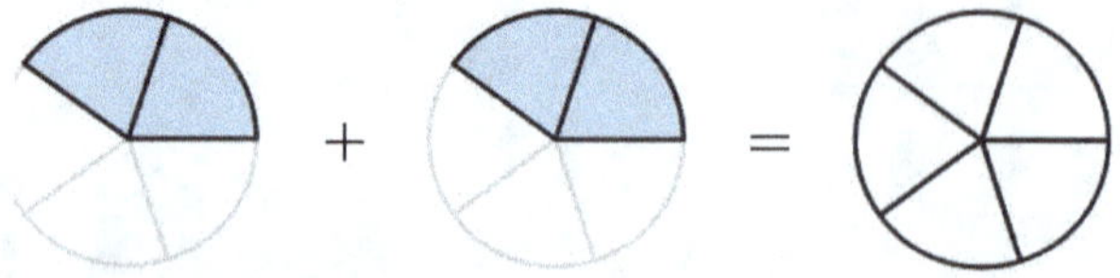     +    =

5) 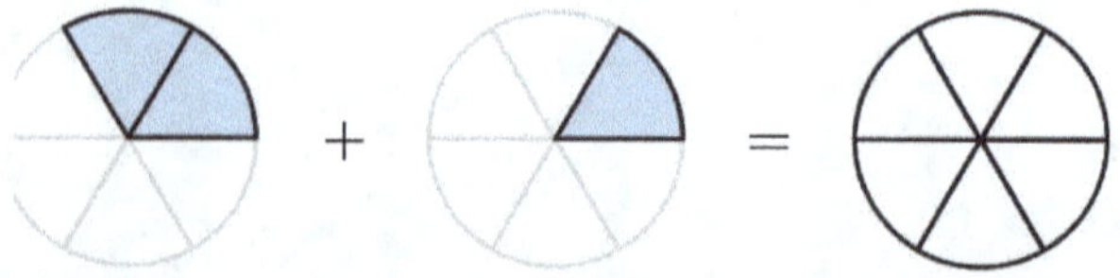     +    =

# SHADE IN THE FRACTION TO SOLVE THE PROBLEM.

1)

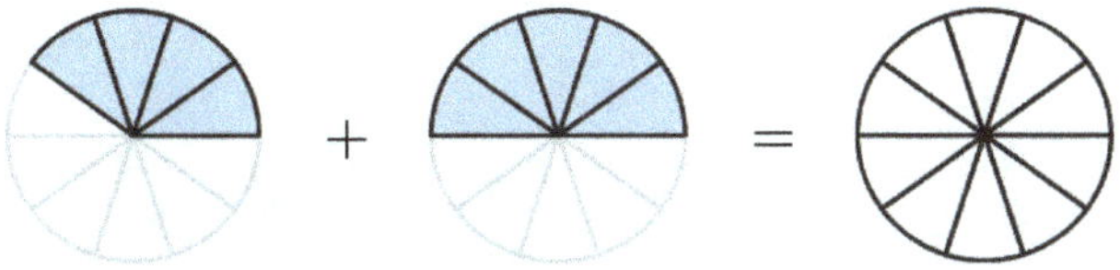

2)

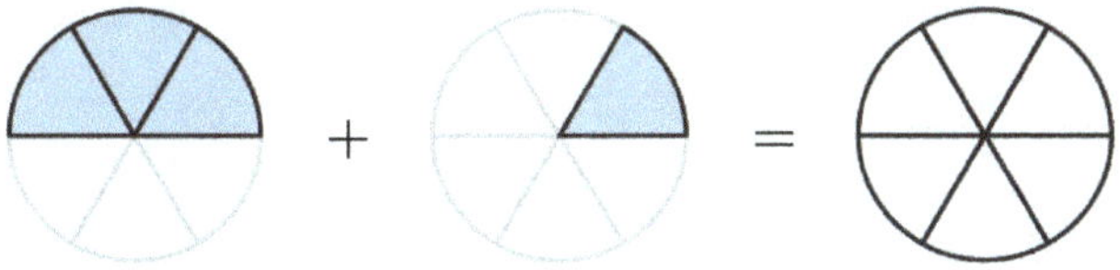

3)

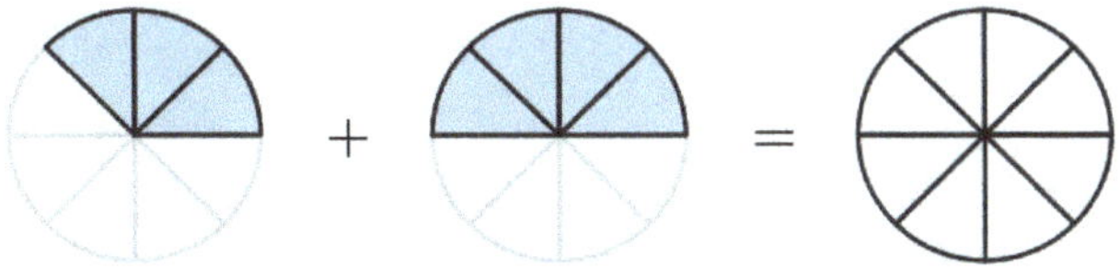

4)

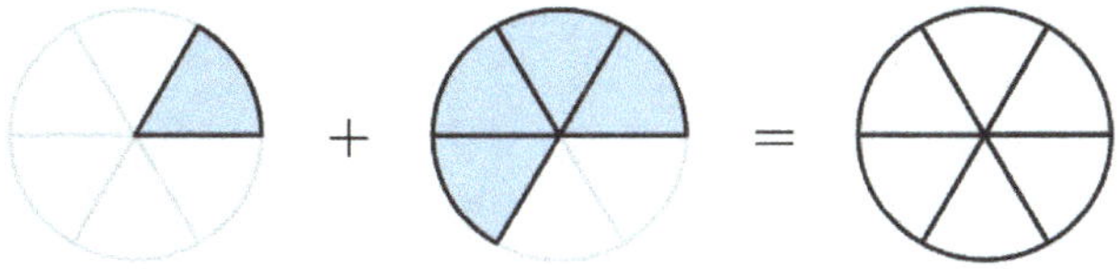

5)

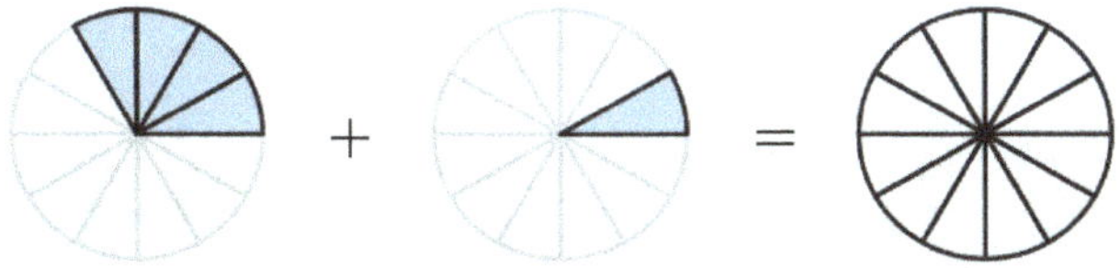

# ADDITION OF FRACTIONS

ACTIVITY NO: **3**

**SHADE IN THE FRACTION TO SOLVE THE PROBLEM.**

1)

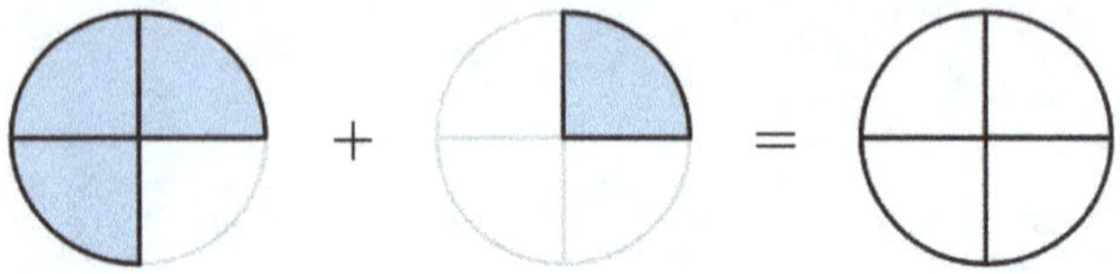

2)

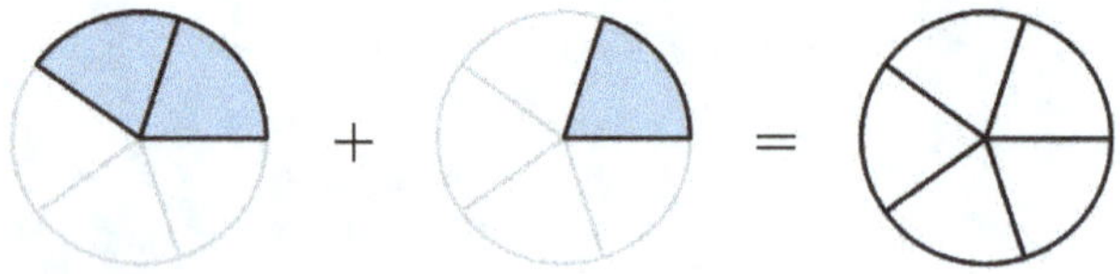

3)

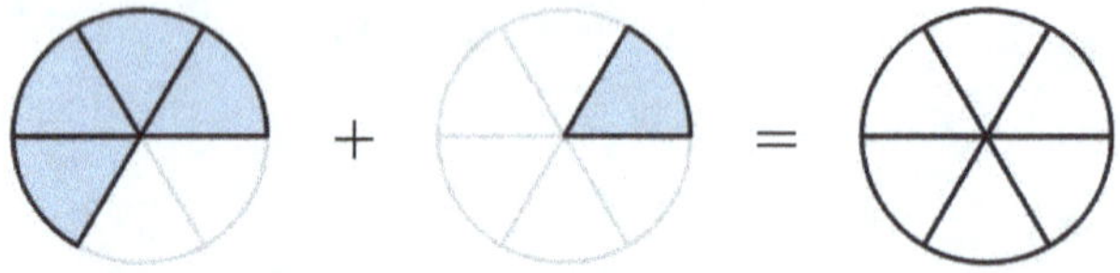

4)

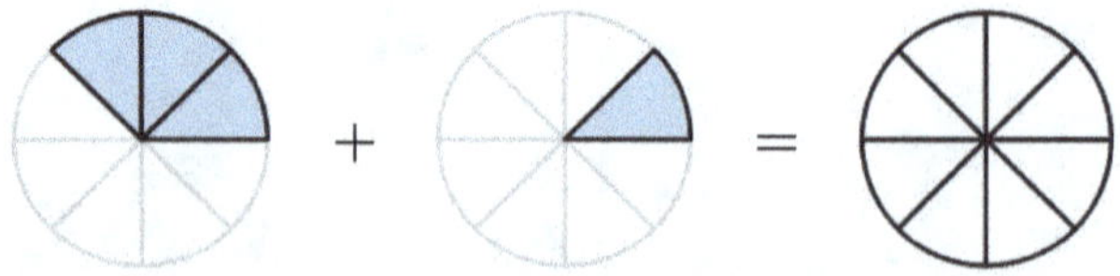

5)

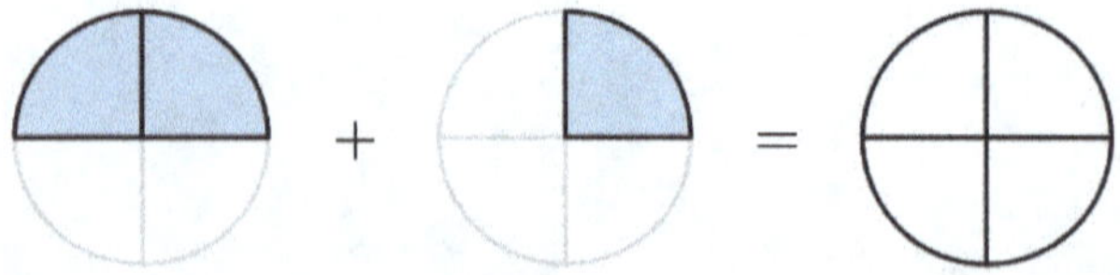

## SHADE IN THE FRACTION TO SOLVE THE PROBLEM.

1) 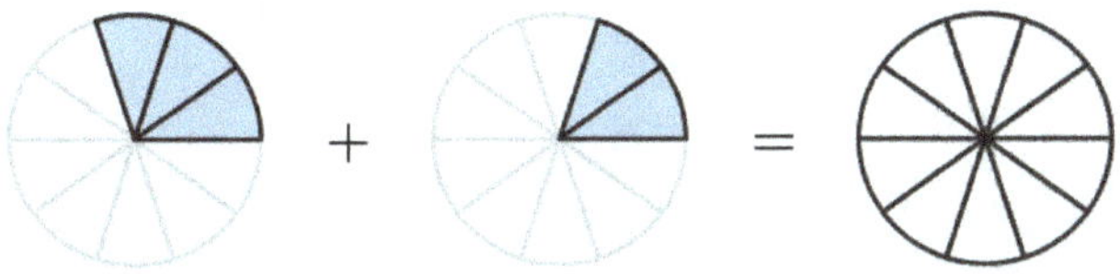 ⬤ + ⬤ = ⬤

2) 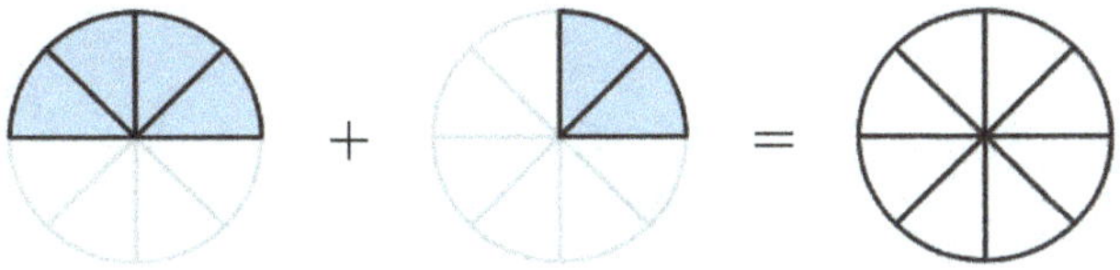 ⬤ + ⬤ = ⬤

3) 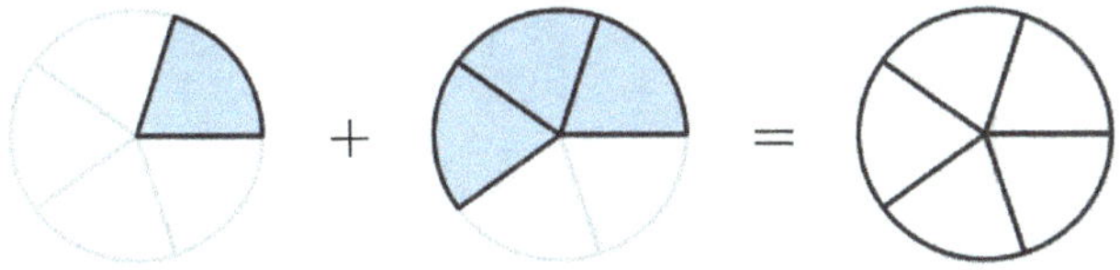 ⬤ + ⬤ = ⬤

4) 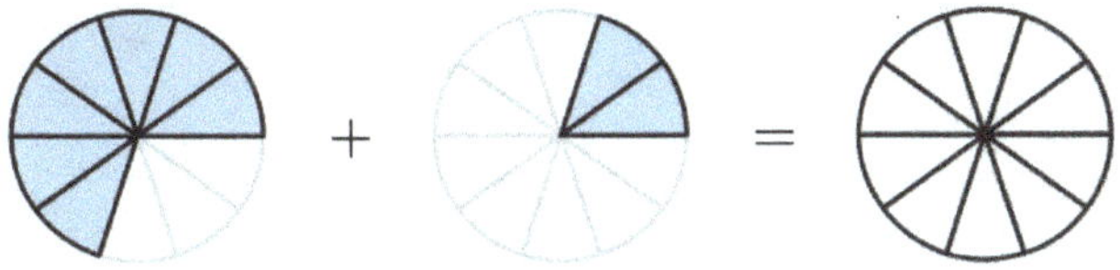 ⬤ + ⬤ = ⬤

5) 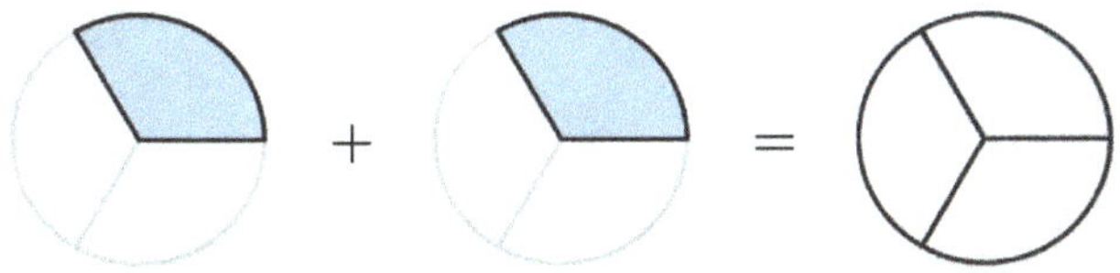 ⬤ + ⬤ = ⬤

**SHADE IN THE FRACTION TO SOLVE THE PROBLEM.**

1) 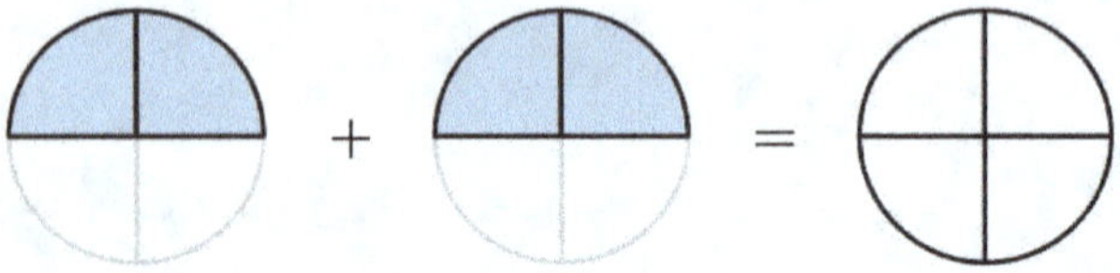  ◯ + ◯ = ◯

2) 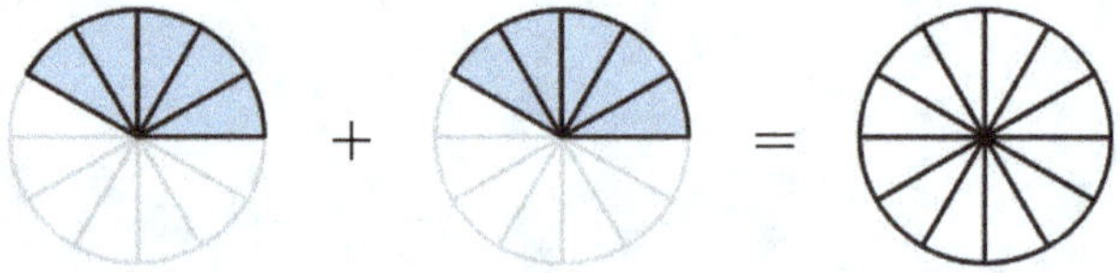  ◯ + ◯ = ◯

3) 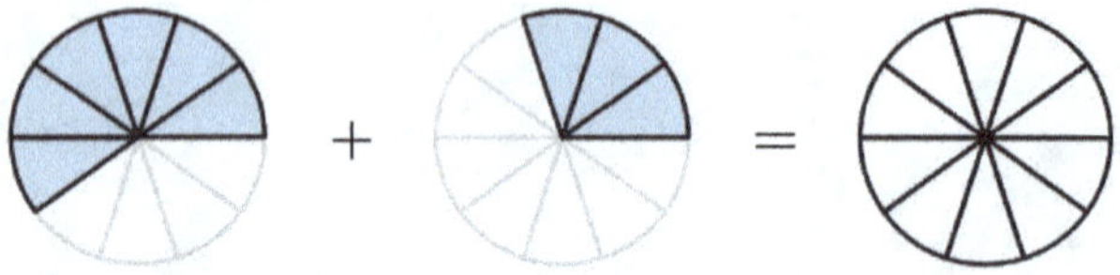  ◯ + ◯ = ◯

4) 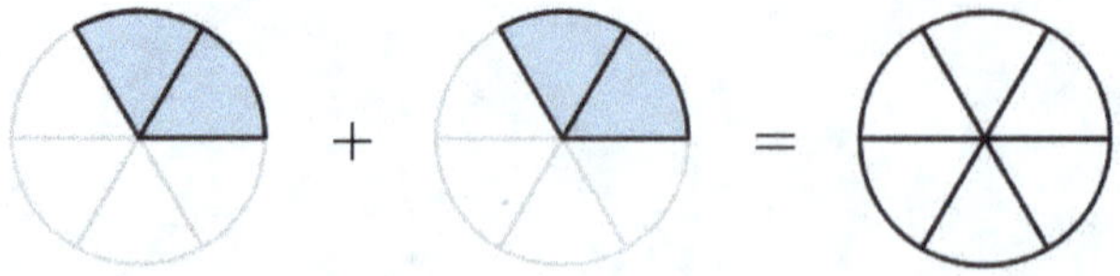  ◯ + ◯ = ◯

5) 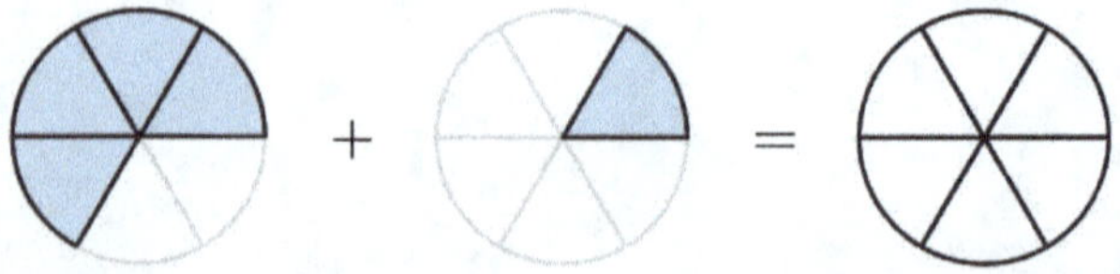  ◯ + ◯ = ◯

## SHADE IN THE FRACTION TO SOLVE THE PROBLEM.

1) 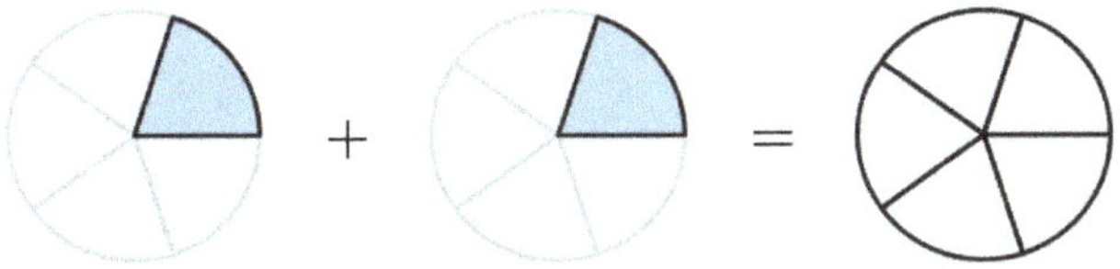 ⬡ + ⬡ = ⬡

2) 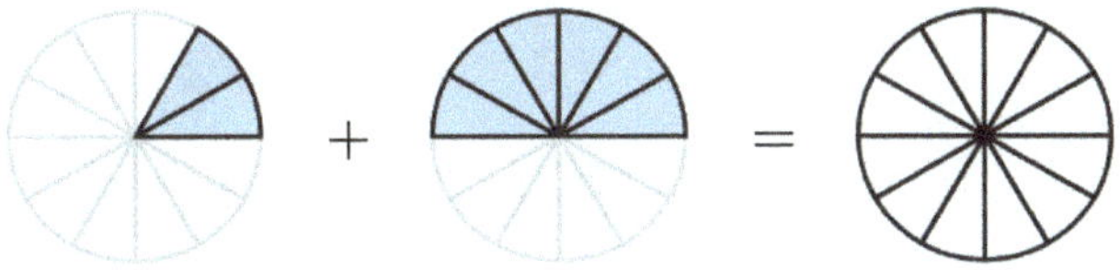 ⬡ + ⬡ = ⬡

3) 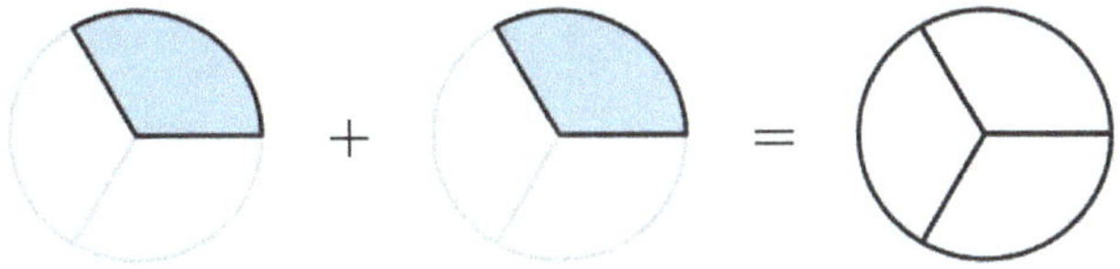 ⬡ + ⬡ = ⬡

4) 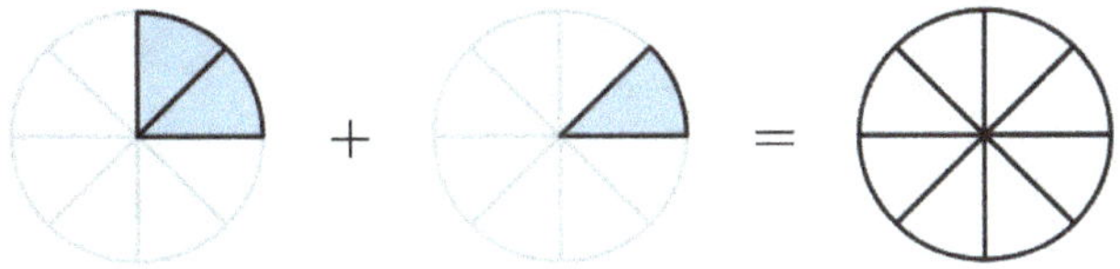 ⬡ + ⬡ = ⬡

5) 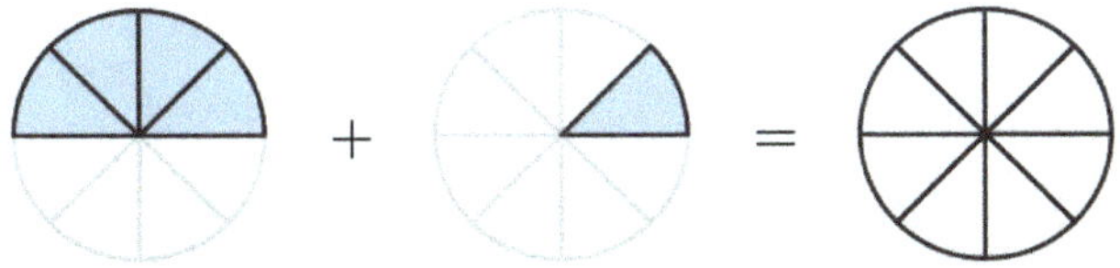 ⬡ + ⬡ = ⬡

**SHADE IN THE FRACTION TO SOLVE THE PROBLEM.**

1)

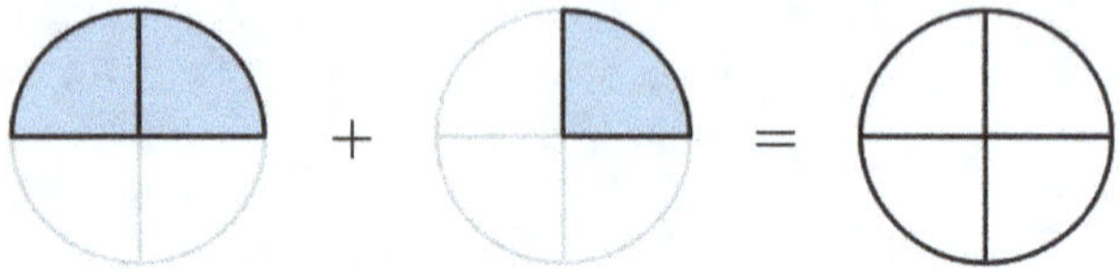

2)

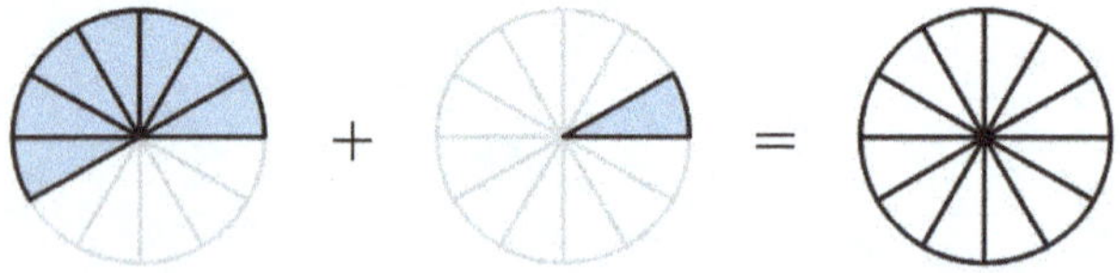

3)

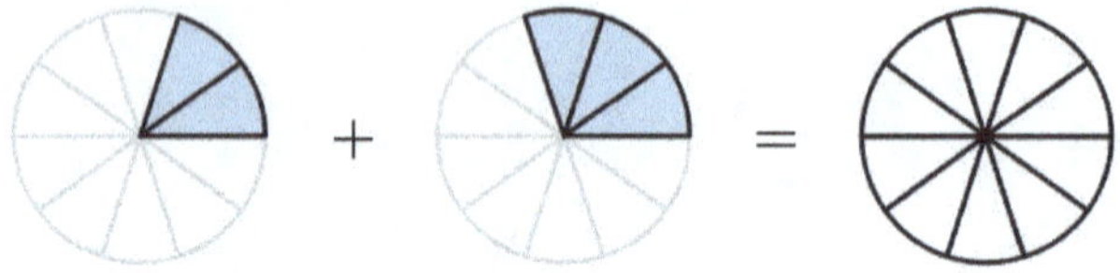

4)

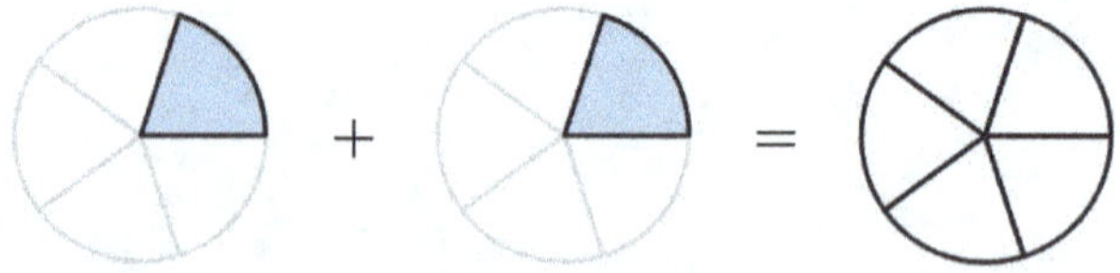

5)

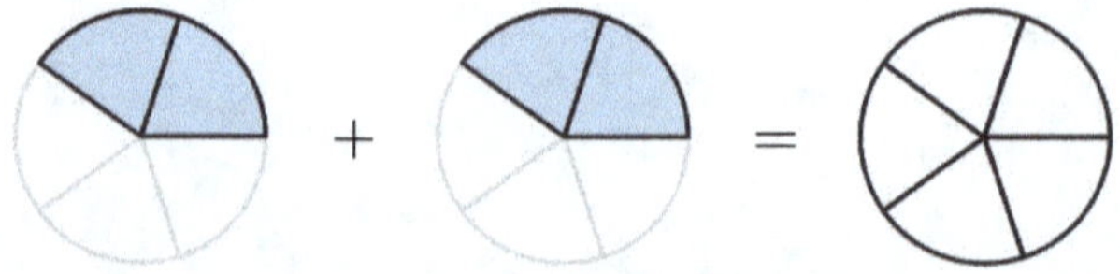

**SHADE IN THE FRACTION TO SOLVE THE PROBLEM.**

1) 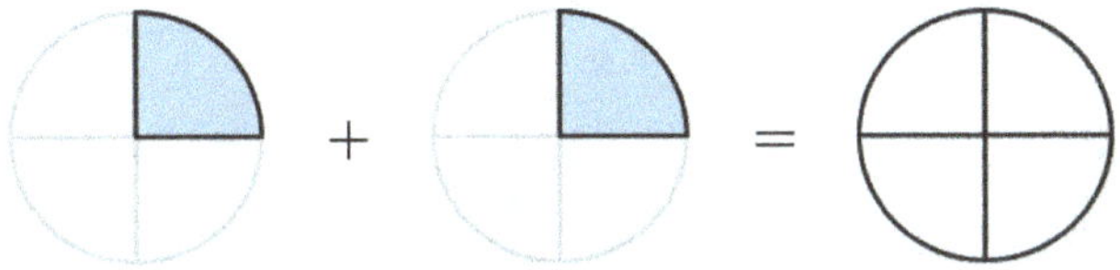 ◯ + ◯ = ◯

2) 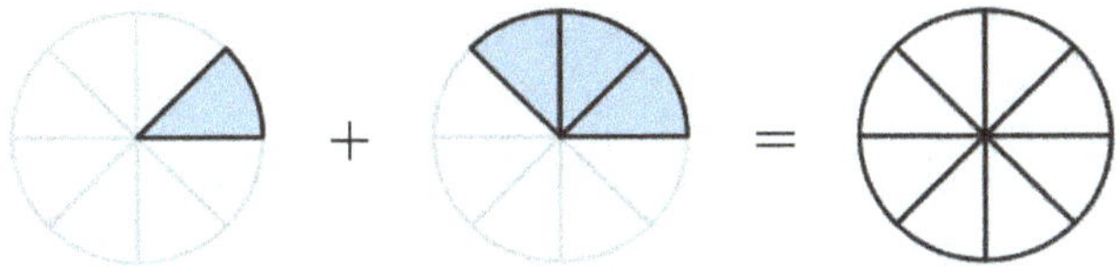 ◯ + ◯ = ◯

3) 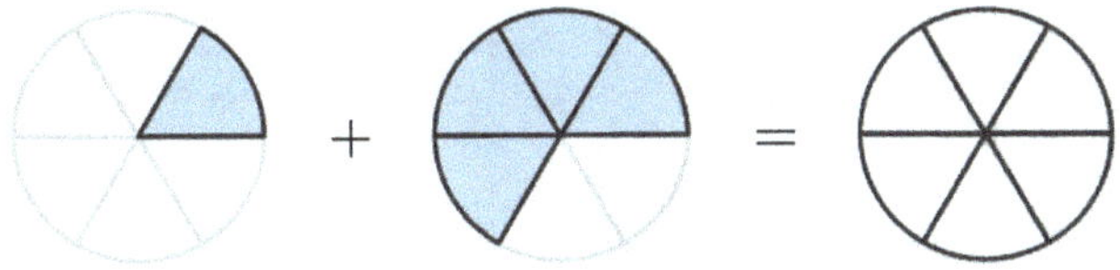 ◯ + ◯ = ◯

4) 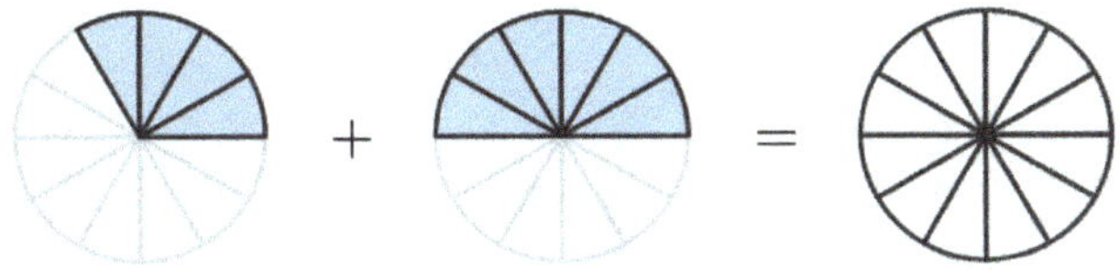 ◯ + ◯ = ◯

5) 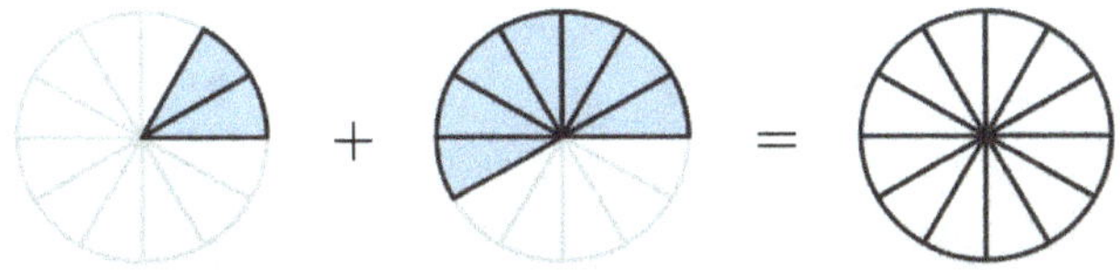 ◯ + ◯ = ◯

# SHADE IN THE FRACTION TO SOLVE THE PROBLEM.

1) 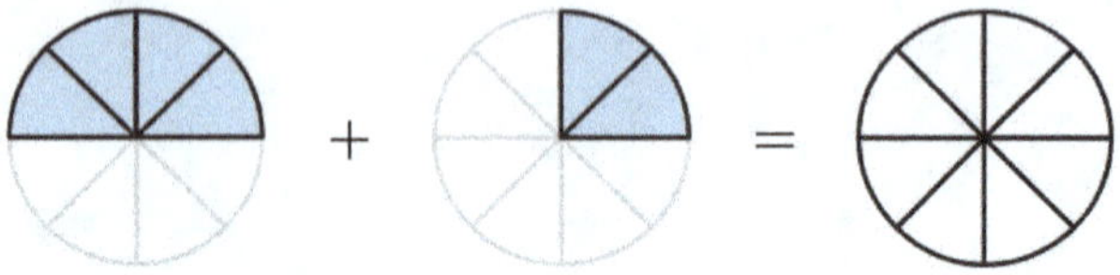    ⬤ + ⬤ = ⬤

2) 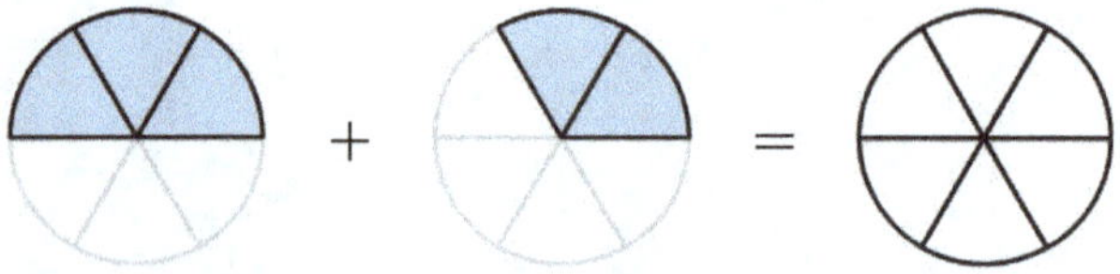    ⬤ + ⬤ = ⬤

3) 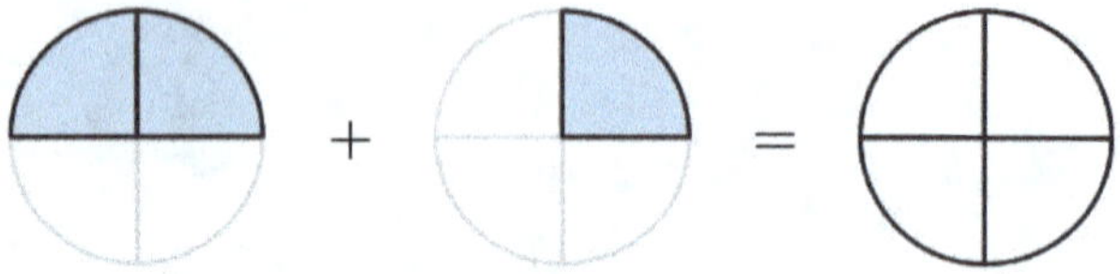    ⬤ + ⬤ = ⬤

4) 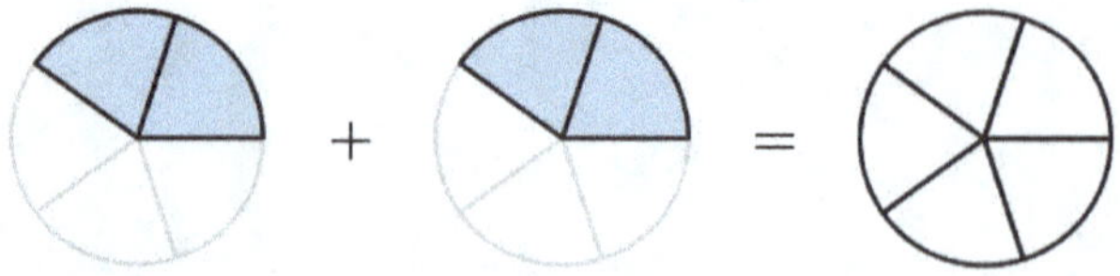    ⬤ + ⬤ = ⬤

5) 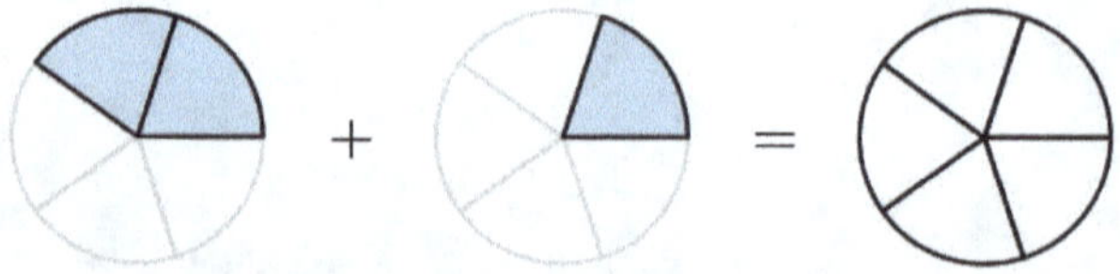    ⬤ + ⬤ = ⬤

SHADE IN THE FRACTION TO SOLVE THE PROBLEM.

1) ◯ + ◯ = ◯

2) ◯ + ◯ = ◯

3) ◯ + ◯ = ◯

4) ◯ + ◯ = ◯

5) ◯ + ◯ = ◯

# SUBTRACTION OF FRACTIONS
## Visual

# SUBTRACTION OF FRACTIONS

**ACTIVITY NO:** 1

SOLVE THE PROBLEMS BELOW AND WRITE THE SIMPLIFIED ANSWERS IN THE SPACE PROVIDED.

**1)** $\frac{5}{6} - \frac{1}{3} =$

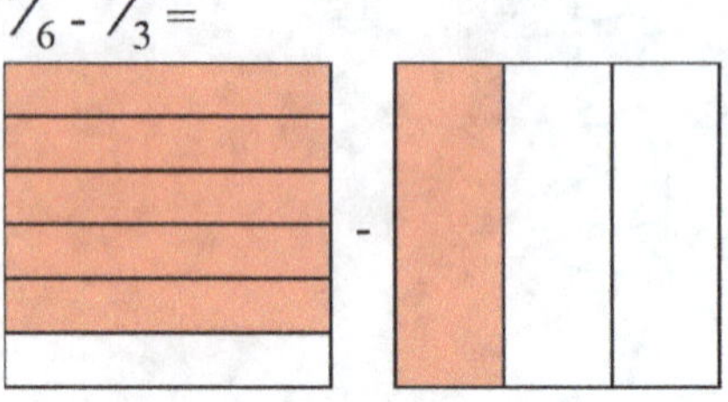

**4)** $\frac{3}{5} - \frac{1}{2} =$

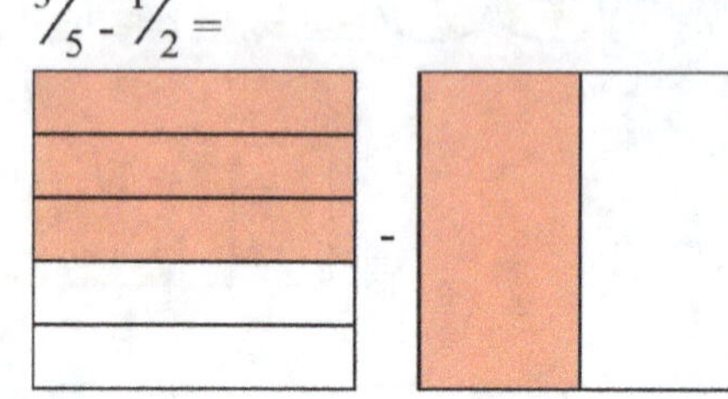

**2)** $\frac{5}{7} - \frac{3}{9} =$

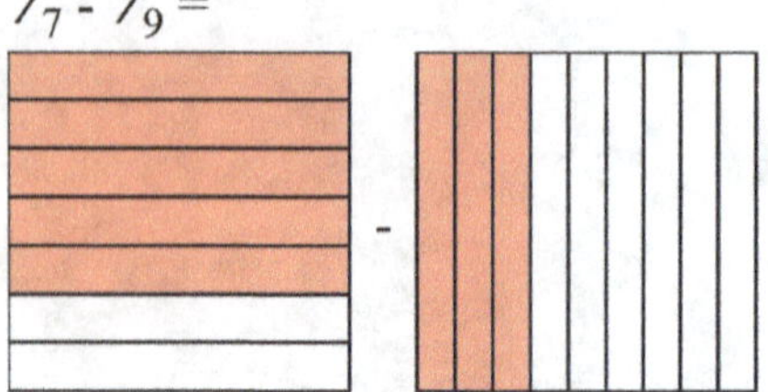

**5)** $\frac{4}{8} - \frac{1}{2} =$

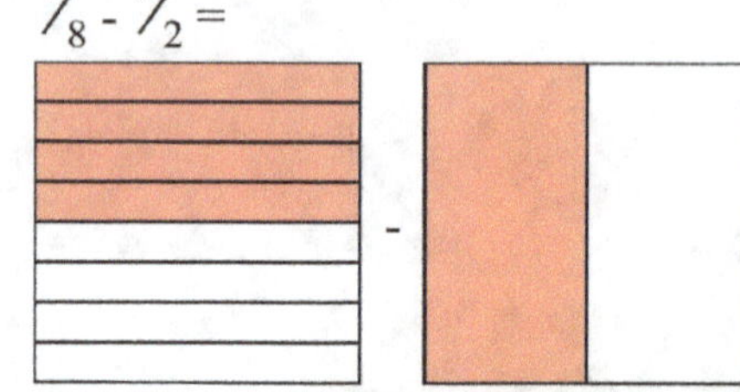

**3)** $\frac{4}{5} - \frac{3}{6} =$

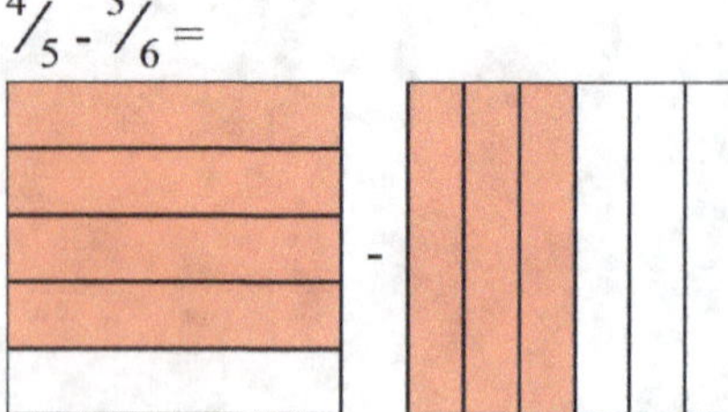

WRITE THE SIMPLIFIED AN-
SWERS HERE:

1. _____________

2. _____________

3. _____________

4. _____________

5. _____________

# SUBTRACTION OF FRACTIONS

**ACTIVITY NO: 2**

SOLVE THE PROBLEMS BELOW AND WRITE THE SIMPLIFIED ANSWERS IN THE SPACE PROVIDED.

**1)** $\frac{7}{9} - \frac{3}{4} =$

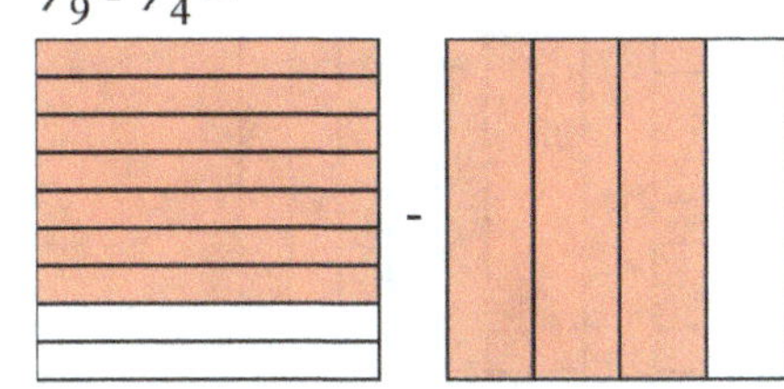

**2)** $\frac{1}{2} - \frac{2}{5} =$

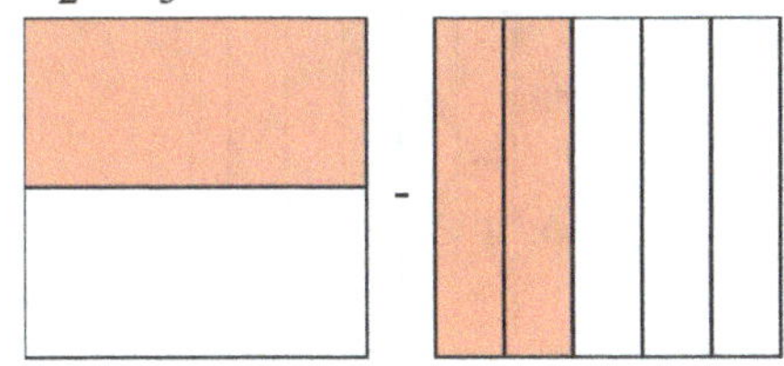

**3)** $\frac{2}{6} - \frac{1}{3} =$

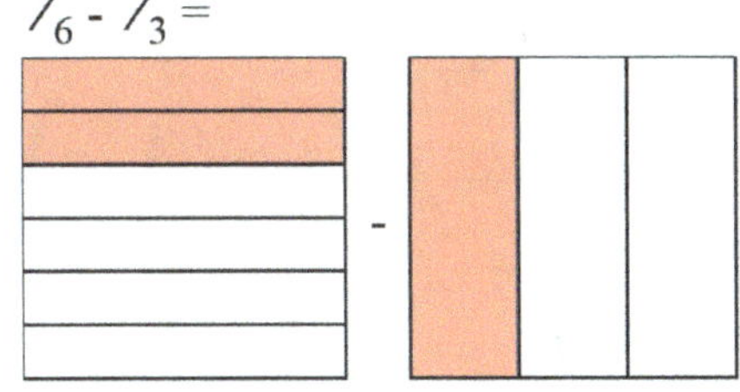

**4)** $\frac{4}{5} - \frac{1}{2} =$

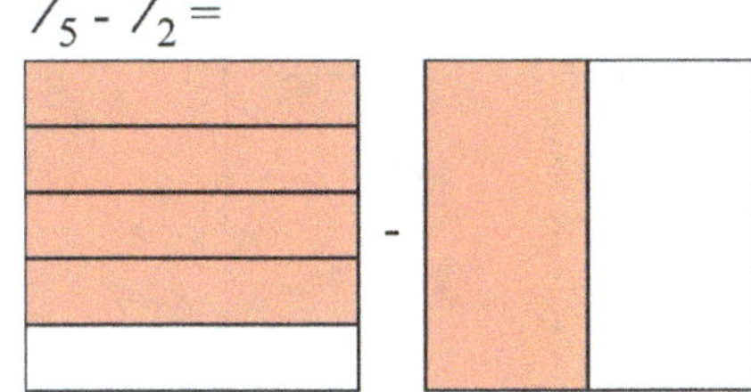

**5)** $\frac{5}{7} - \frac{1}{2} =$

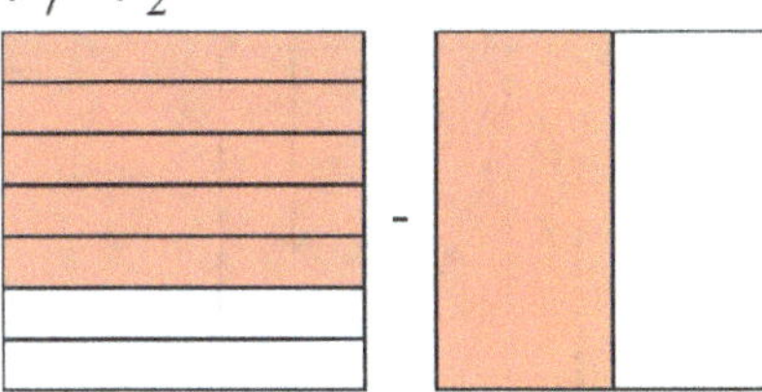

WRITE THE SIMPLIFIED ANSWERS HERE:

1. __________
2. __________
3. __________
4. __________
5. __________

# SUBTRACTION OF FRACTIONS

ACTIVITY NO: **3**

SOLVE THE PROBLEMS BELOW AND WRITE THE SIMPLIFIED ANSWERS IN THE SPACE PROVIDED.

1) $\frac{2}{4} - \frac{1}{2} =$

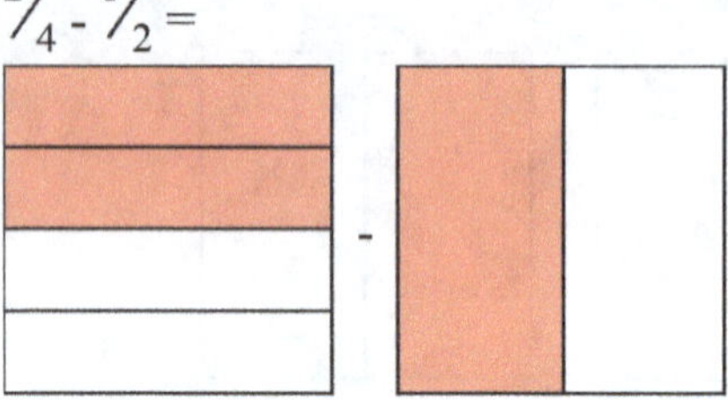

4) $\frac{7}{8} - \frac{2}{7} =$

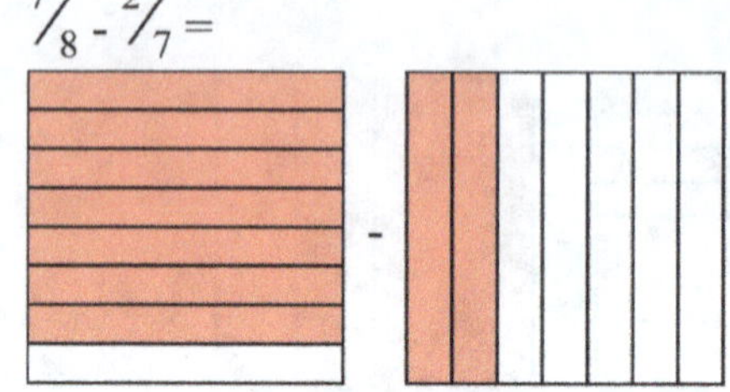

2) $\frac{4}{8} - \frac{2}{5} =$

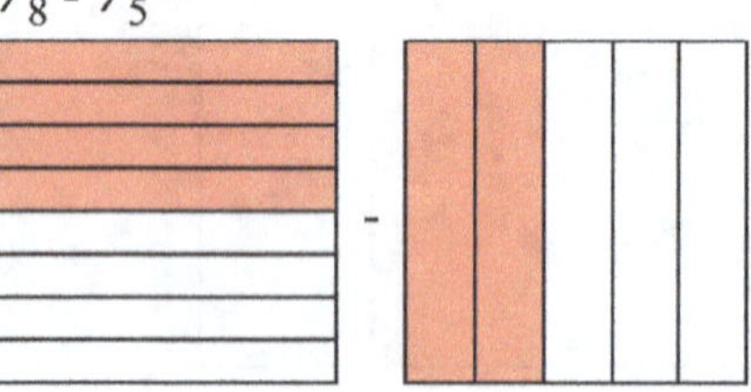

5) $\frac{8}{9} - \frac{3}{6} =$

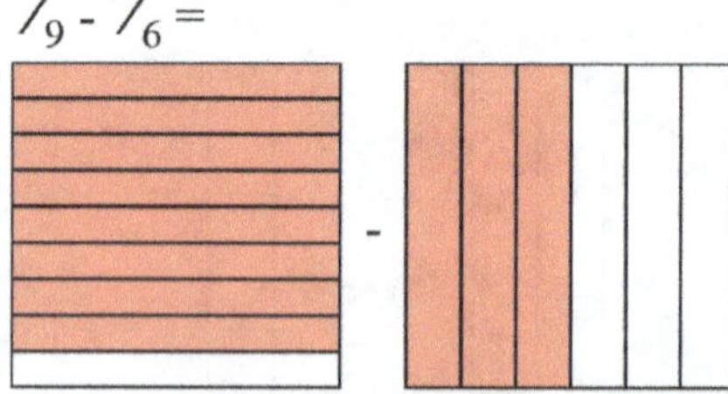

3) $\frac{5}{7} - \frac{5}{8} =$

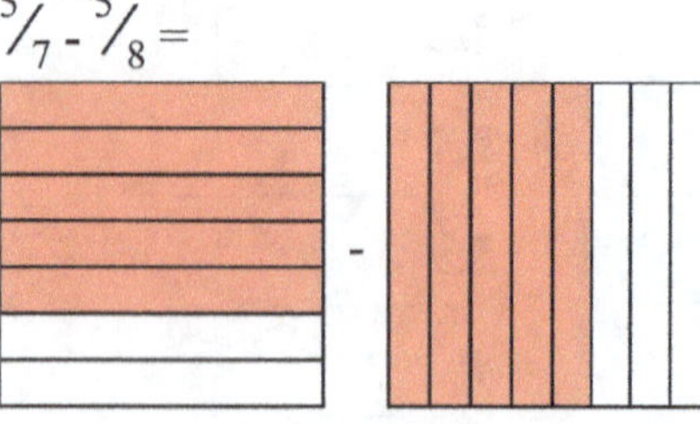

WRITE THE SIMPLIFIED ANSWERS HERE:

1. _______________

2. _______________

3. _______________

4. _______________

5. _______________

SOLVE THE PROBLEMS BELOW AND WRITE THE SIMPLIFIED ANSWERS IN THE SPACE PROVIDED.

1) $\frac{4}{5} - \frac{1}{6} =$

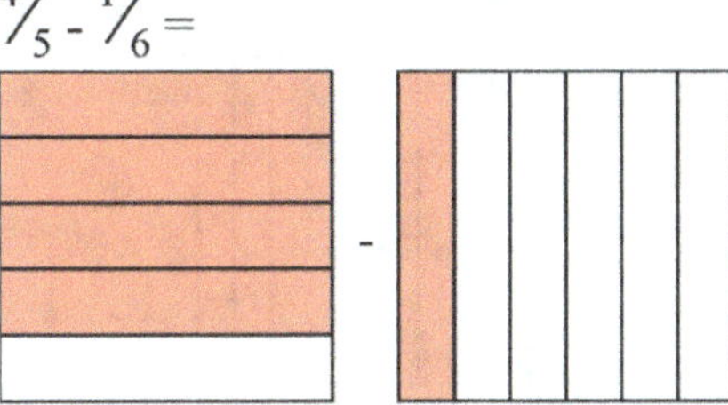

4) $\frac{1}{6} - \frac{1}{9} =$

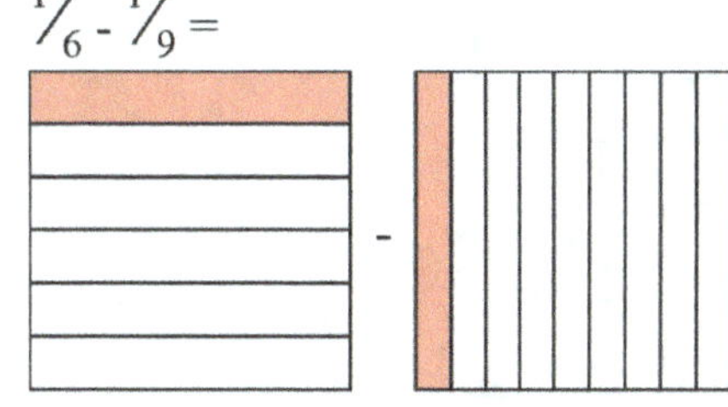

2) $\frac{5}{6} - \frac{7}{10} =$

5) $\frac{1}{2} - \frac{1}{7} =$

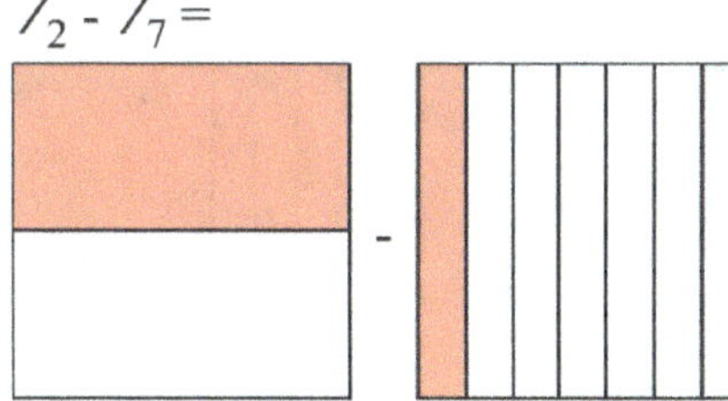

3) $\frac{3}{5} - \frac{1}{10} =$

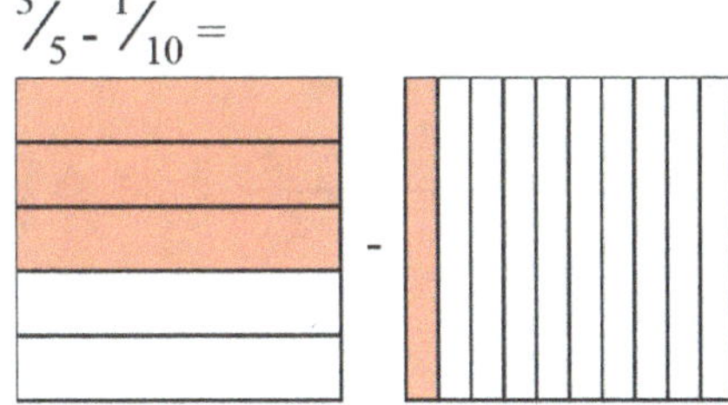

WRITE THE SIMPLIFIED ANSWERS HERE:

1. __________

2. __________

3. __________

4. __________

5. __________

# SUBTRACTION OF FRACTIONS

**ACTIVITY NO:** **5**

**SOLVE THE PROBLEMS BELOW AND WRITE THE SIMPLIFIED ANSWERS IN THE SPACE PROVIDED.**

**1)** $\frac{6}{10} - \frac{1}{2} =$

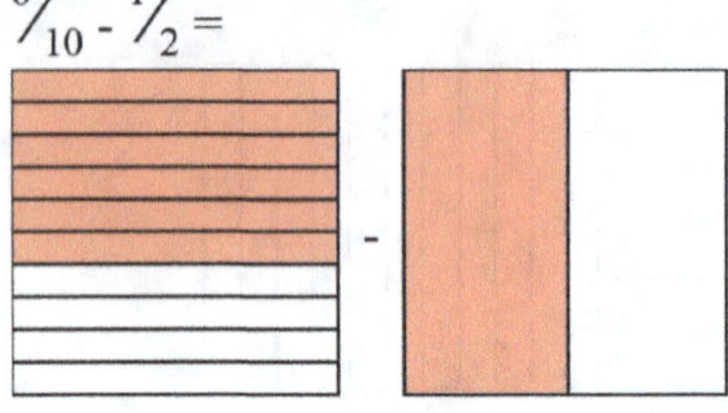

**4)** $\frac{1}{2} - \frac{3}{9} =$

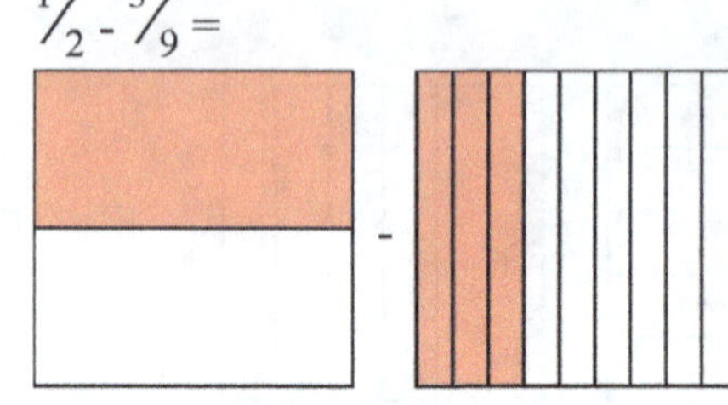

**2)** $\frac{8}{10} - \frac{1}{8} =$

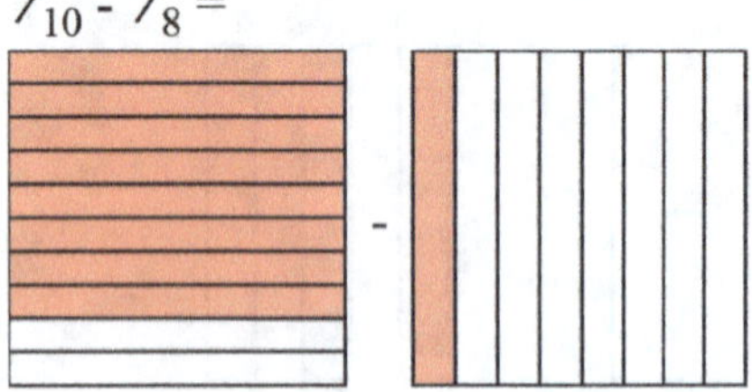

**5)** $\frac{2}{5} - \frac{1}{3} =$

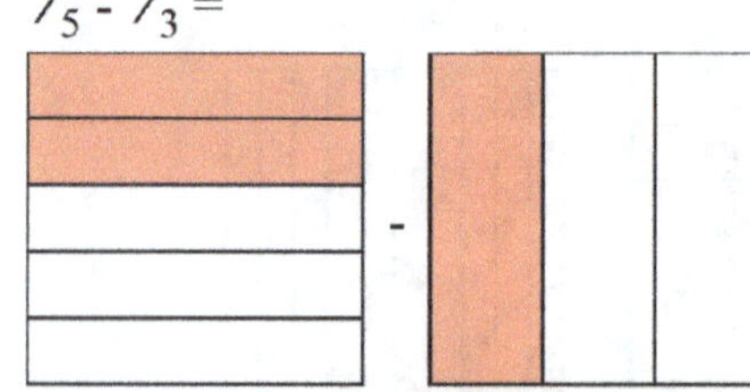

**3)** $\frac{4}{5} - \frac{3}{4} =$

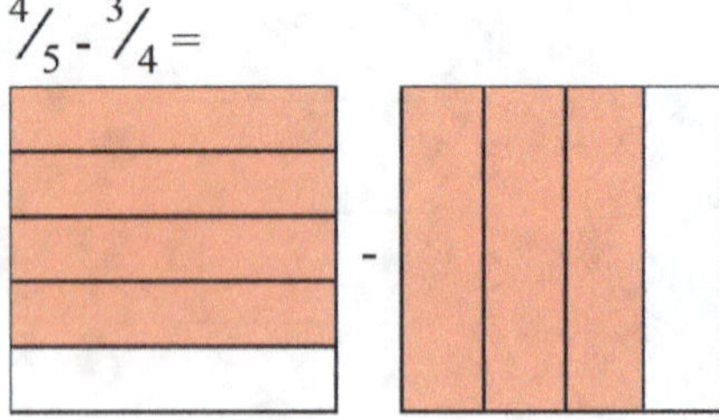

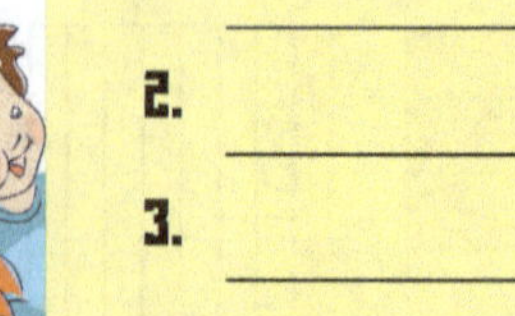

**WRITE THE SIMPLIFIED ANSWERS HERE:**

1. _______________
2. _______________
3. _______________
4. _______________
5. _______________

**SOLVE THE PROBLEMS BELOW AND WRITE THE SIMPLIFIED ANSWERS IN THE SPACE PROVIDED.**

1) $\frac{8}{10} - \frac{4}{5} =$

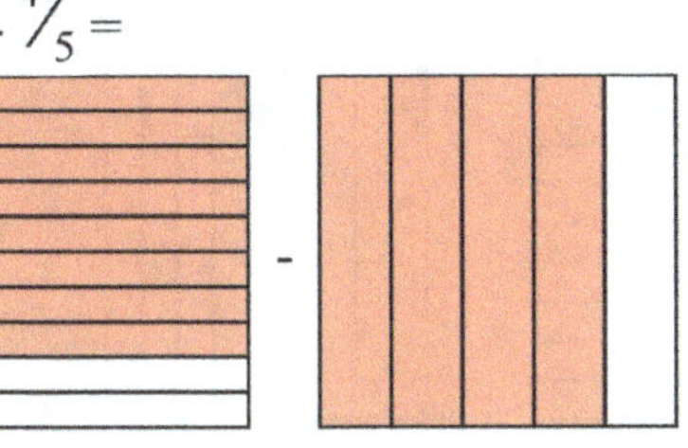

4) $\frac{1}{2} - \frac{3}{7} =$

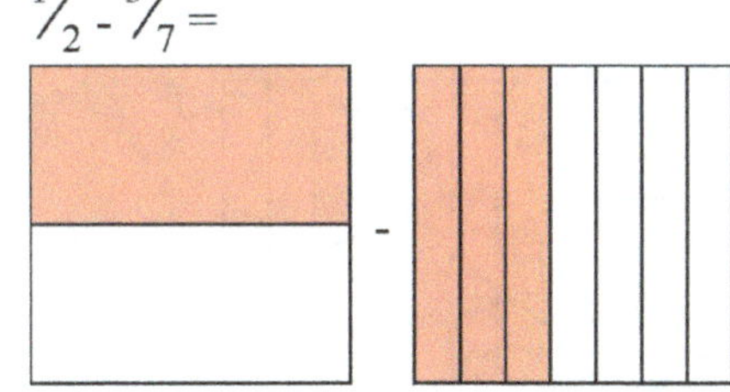

2) $\frac{2}{3} - \frac{2}{6} =$

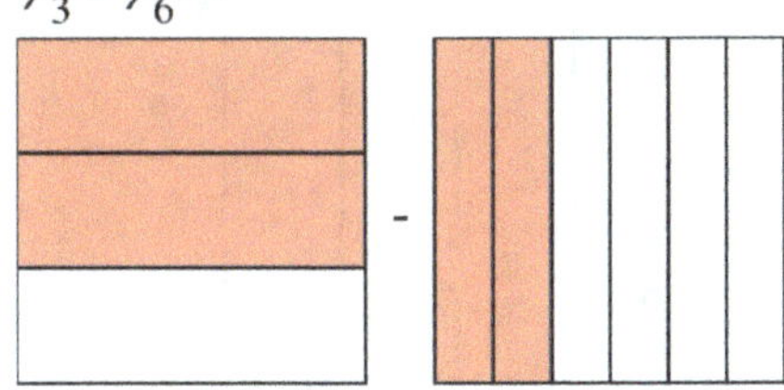

5) $\frac{6}{8} - \frac{1}{4} =$

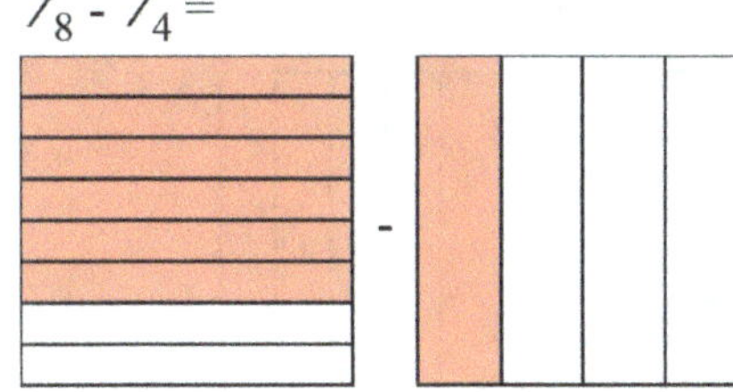

3) $\frac{3}{4} - \frac{6}{10} =$

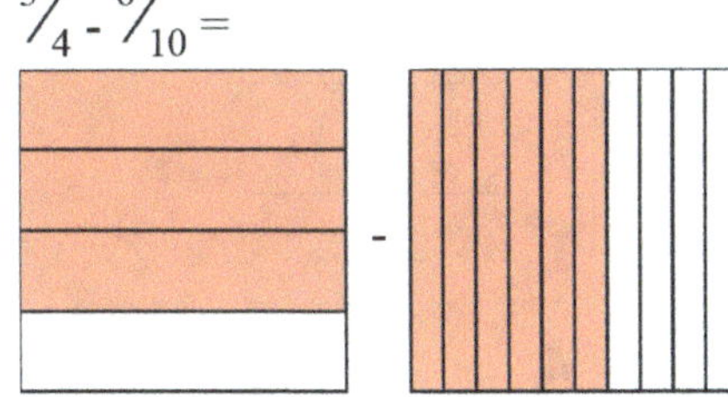

**WRITE THE SIMPLIFIED ANSWERS HERE:**

1. _______________

2. _______________

3. _______________

4. _______________

5. _______________

# SUBTRACTION OF FRACTIONS



SOLVE THE PROBLEMS BELOW AND WRITE THE SIMPLIFIED ANSWERS IN THE SPACE PROVIDED.

1) $\frac{7}{8} - \frac{5}{7} =$

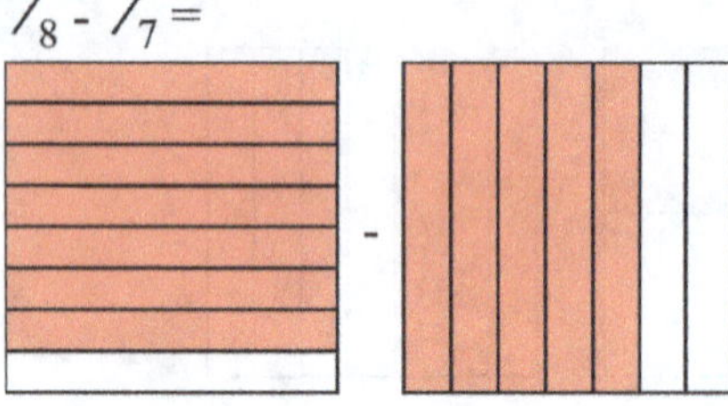

4) $\frac{5}{9} - \frac{2}{10} =$

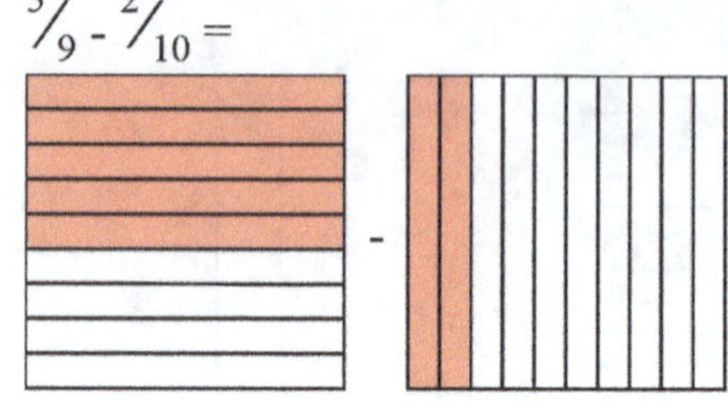

2) $\frac{9}{10} - \frac{2}{6} =$

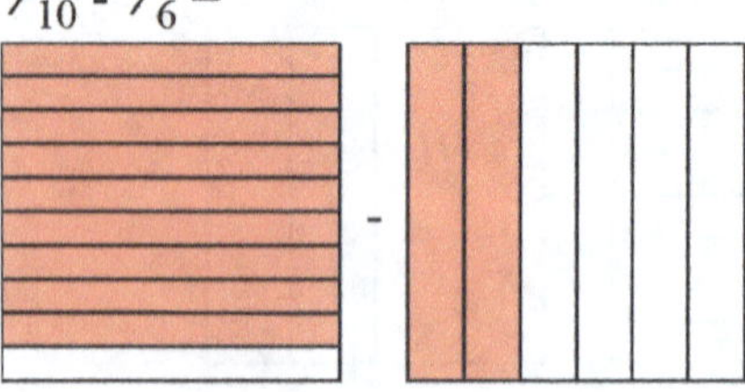

5) $\frac{6}{8} - \frac{2}{3} =$

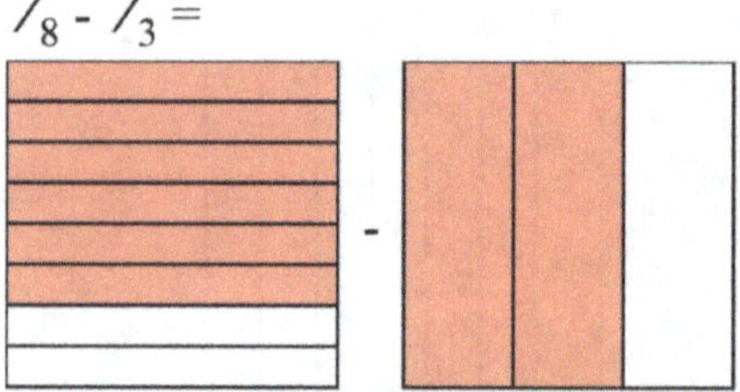

3) $\frac{2}{7} - \frac{2}{10} =$

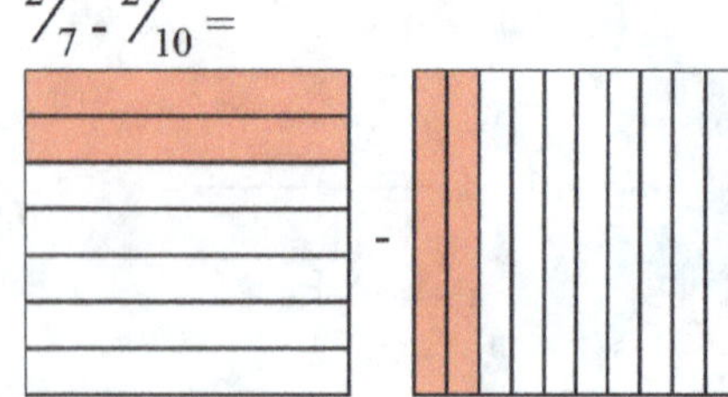

WRITE THE SIMPLIFIED ANSWERS HERE:

1. __________
2. __________
3. __________
4. __________
5. __________

# SUBTRACTION OF FRACTIONS

SOLVE THE PROBLEMS BELOW AND WRITE THE SIMPLIFIED ANSWERS IN THE SPACE PROVIDED.

1) $\frac{2}{5} - \frac{1}{3} =$

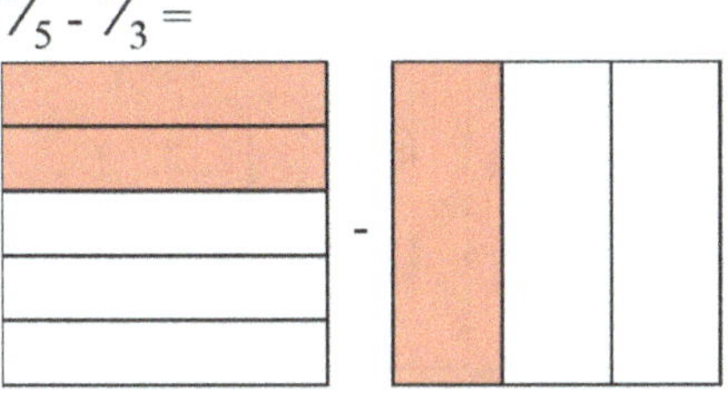

4) $\frac{4}{5} - \frac{1}{4} =$

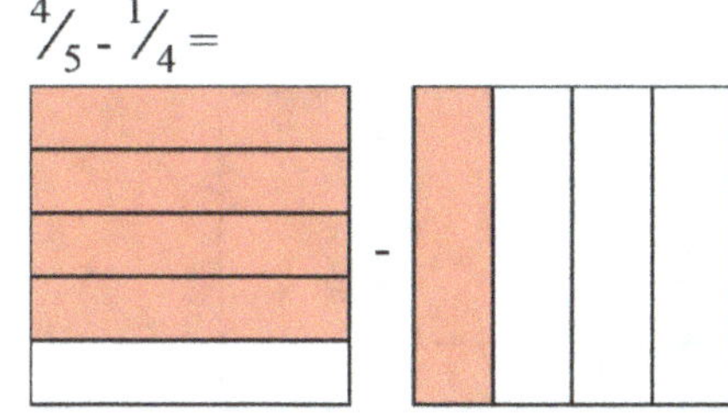

2) $\frac{7}{8} - \frac{1}{2} =$

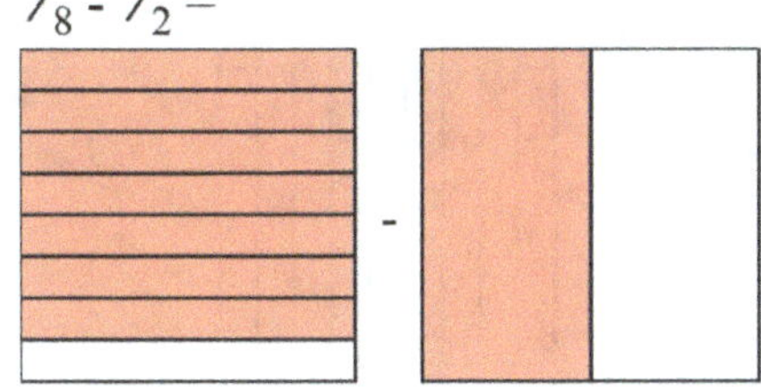

5) $\frac{1}{2} - \frac{2}{5} =$

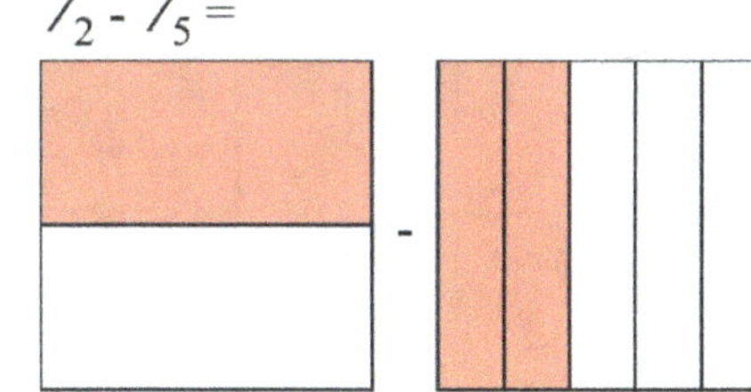

3) $\frac{8}{9} - \frac{3}{10} =$

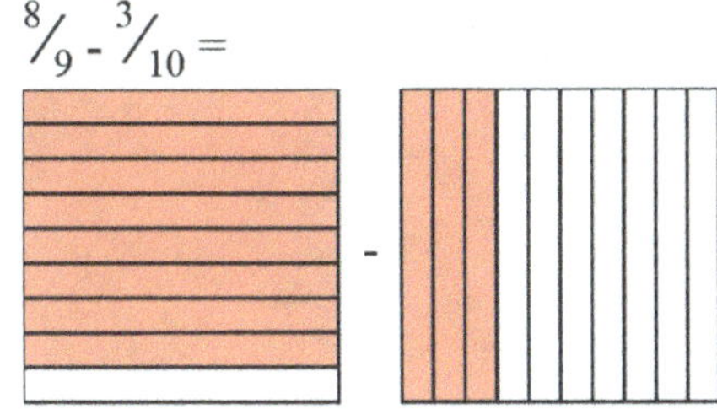

WRITE THE SIMPLIFIED ANSWERS HERE:

1. _______________

2. _______________

3. _______________

4. _______________

5. _______________

# SUBTRACTION OF FRACTIONS

SOLVE THE PROBLEMS BELOW AND WRITE THE SIMPLIFIED ANSWERS IN THE SPACE PROVIDED.

1) $\frac{3}{5} - \frac{1}{2} =$

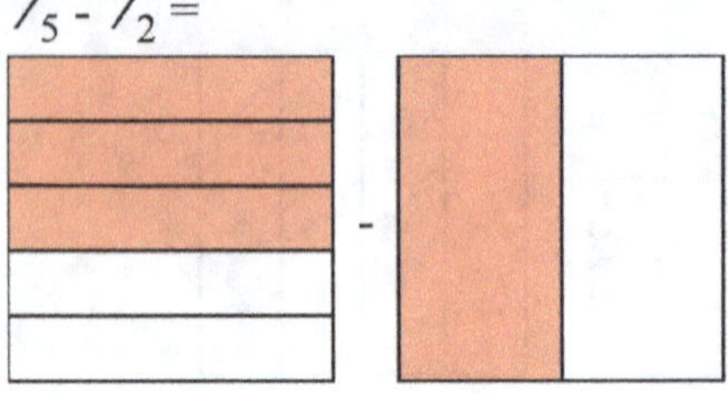

2) $\frac{3}{7} - \frac{1}{3} =$

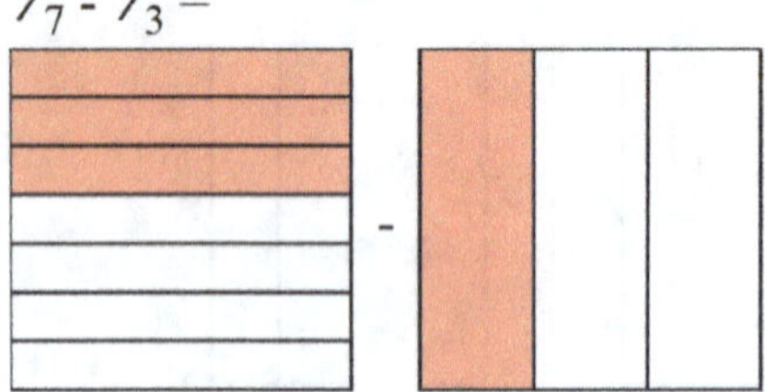

3) $\frac{7}{10} - \frac{2}{7} =$

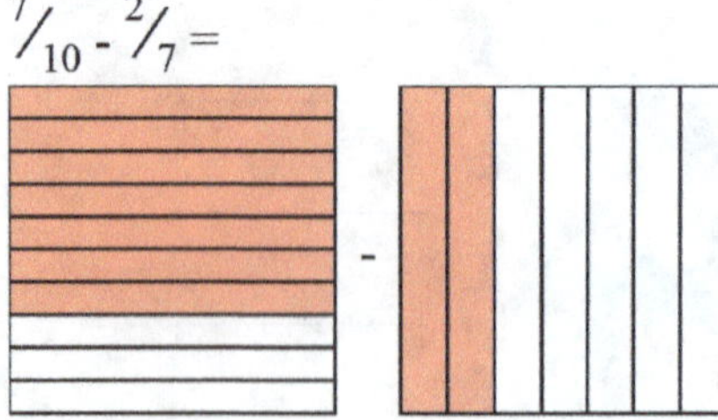

4) $\frac{3}{8} - \frac{1}{6} =$

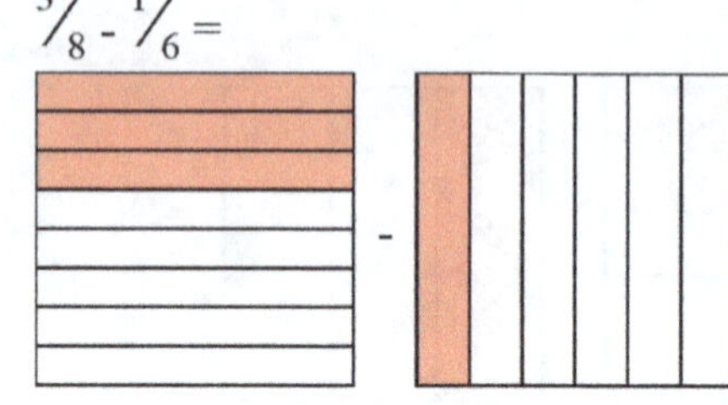

5) $\frac{4}{8} - \frac{3}{9} =$

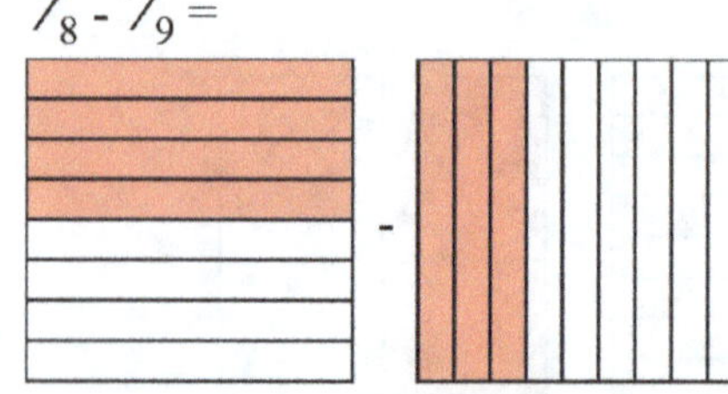

**WRITE THE SIMPLIFIED ANSWERS HERE:**

1. _______________
2. _______________
3. _______________
4. _______________
5. _______________

# SUBTRACTION OF FRACTIONS  ACTIVITY NO: 10

SOLVE THE PROBLEMS BELOW AND WRITE THE SIMPLIFIED ANSWERS IN THE SPACE PROVIDED.

1) $\frac{2}{7} - \frac{1}{9} =$

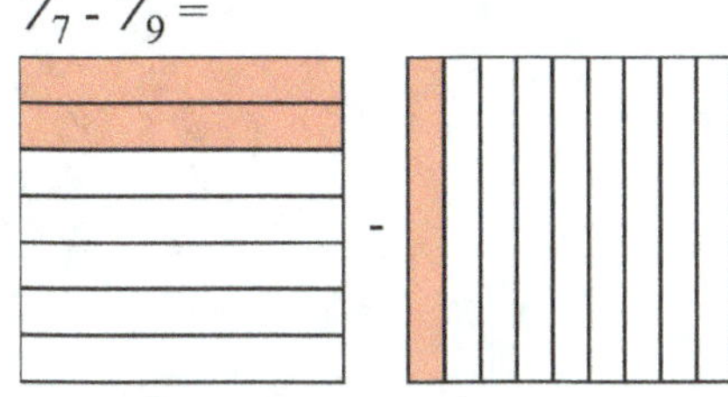

4) $\frac{4}{5} - \frac{6}{9} =$

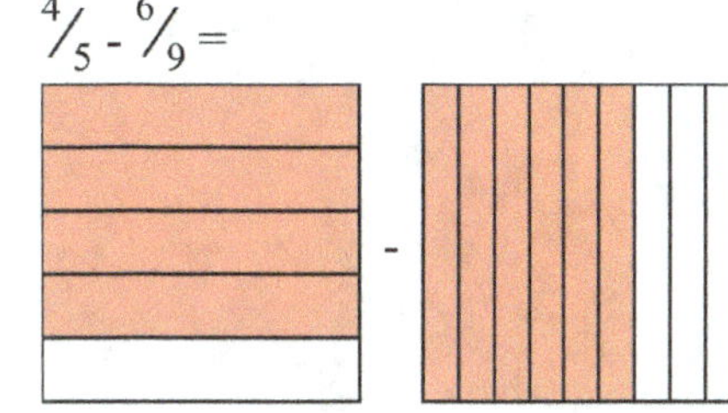

2) $\frac{2}{3} - \frac{4}{8} =$

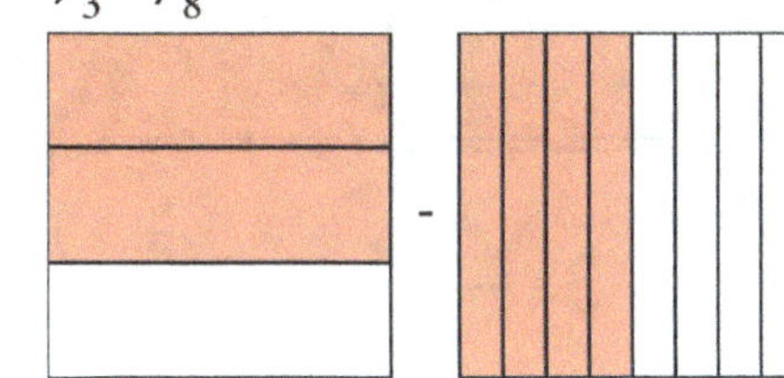

5) $\frac{5}{9} - \frac{1}{7} =$

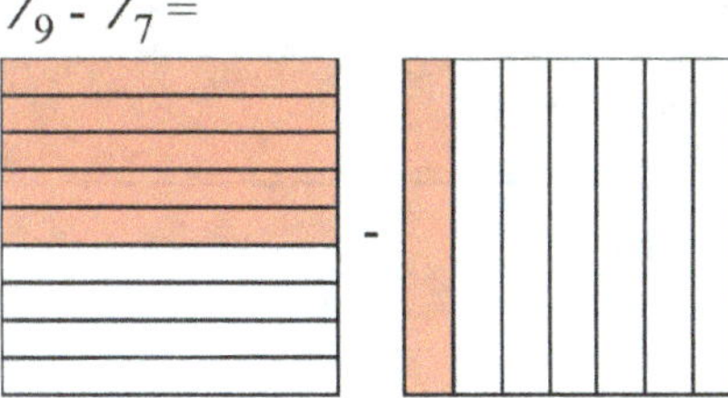

3) $\frac{2}{4} - \frac{1}{2} =$

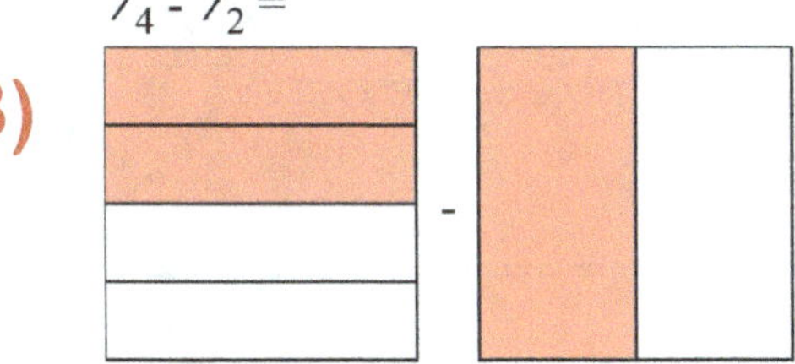

WRITE THE SIMPLIFIED ANSWERS HERE:

1. ____________

2. ____________

3. ____________

4. ____________

5. ____________

# MIXED AND IMPROPER FRACTIONS

## Convert the improper fraction to a mixed number fraction.

$$\frac{17}{5}$$

First divide the numerator by the denominator.

$17 \div 5 = 3$ with a remainder of 2

$$3 \frac{2}{5}$$

The 3 is your whole number. While the remainder becomes the numerator.

$$3 \frac{2}{5}$$

Your denominator stays the same.
And now you have your mixed number.

# Convert the mixed number fraction to an improper fraction

$$3 \frac{2}{5}$$

First multiply the denominator by the whole number.

$5 \times 3 = 15$

$$3 \frac{17}{5}$$

Next add your answer from step 1 to your numerator.

$$\frac{17}{5}$$

Finally drop the whole number. Now you have your improper fraction.

## SIMPLIFY THE FRACTIONS BELOW. WRITE YOUR ANSWERS IN THE SPACE PROVIDED.

1] $\dfrac{35}{4} =$     2] $\dfrac{37}{5} =$     3] $\dfrac{13}{7} =$

4] $\dfrac{5}{2} =$     5] $\dfrac{28}{3} =$     6] $\dfrac{25}{3} =$

7] $\dfrac{65}{7} =$     8] $\dfrac{32}{6} =$     9] $\dfrac{36}{5} =$

**WRITE THE SIMPLIFIED ANSWERS HERE:**

1. _______      4. _______      7. _______

2. _______      5. _______      8. _______

3. _______      6. _______      9. _______

# 2

## SIMPLIFY THE FRACTIONS BELOW. WRITE YOUR ANSWERS IN THE SPACE PROVIDED.

1] $\dfrac{64}{7} =$        2] $\dfrac{12}{7} =$        3] $\dfrac{42}{5} =$

4] $\dfrac{79}{8} =$        5] $\dfrac{66}{7} =$        6] $\dfrac{68}{8} =$

7] $\dfrac{3}{2} =$        8] $\dfrac{19}{3} =$        9] $\dfrac{38}{4} =$

**WRITE THE SIMPLIFIED ANSWERS HERE:**

1. _____________      4. _____________     7. _____________

2. _____________      5. _____________     8. _____________

3. _____________      6. _____________     9. _____________

## SIMPLIFY THE FRACTIONS BELOW. WRITE YOUR ANSWERS IN THE SPACE PROVIDED.

1] $\dfrac{32}{5} =$

2] $\dfrac{55}{7} =$

3] $\dfrac{18}{4} =$

4] $\dfrac{13}{2} =$

5] $\dfrac{19}{2} =$

6] $\dfrac{24}{9} =$

7] $\dfrac{55}{6} =$

8] $\dfrac{8}{7} =$

9] $\dfrac{9}{4} =$

**WRITE THE SIMPLIFIED ANSWERS HERE:**

1. __________

2. __________

3. __________

4. __________

5. __________

6. __________

7. __________

8. __________

9. __________

## SIMPLIFY THE FRACTIONS BELOW. WRITE YOUR ANSWERS IN THE SPACE PROVIDED.

1] $\dfrac{5}{3} =$ 

2] $\dfrac{17}{4} =$ 

3] $\dfrac{42}{4} =$ 

4] $\dfrac{13}{3} =$ 

5] $\dfrac{74}{8} =$ 

6] $\dfrac{11}{2} =$ 

7] $\dfrac{52}{7} =$ 

8] $\dfrac{16}{3} =$ 

9] $\dfrac{39}{8} =$ 

**WRITE THE SIMPLIFIED ANSWERS HERE:**

1. ___________

2. ___________

3. ___________

4. ___________

5. ___________

6. ___________

7. ___________

8. ___________

9. ___________

SIMPLIFY THE FRACTIONS BELOW. WRITE YOUR ANSWERS IN THE SPACE PROVIDED.

1] $\dfrac{5}{2} =$

2] $\dfrac{32}{3} =$

3] $\dfrac{29}{7} =$

4] $\dfrac{13}{2} =$

5] $\dfrac{19}{4} =$

6] $\dfrac{39}{10} =$

7] $\dfrac{17}{9} =$

8] $\dfrac{11}{6} =$

9] $\dfrac{15}{10} =$

WRITE THE SIMPLIFIED ANSWERS HERE:

1. __________

2. __________

3. __________

4. __________

5. __________

6. __________

7. __________

8. __________

9. __________

## SIMPLIFY THE FRACTIONS BELOW. WRITE YOUR ANSWERS IN THE SPACE PROVIDED.

1] $\dfrac{39}{7} =$        2] $\dfrac{9}{2} =$        3] $\dfrac{31}{3} =$

4] $\dfrac{29}{5} =$        5] $\dfrac{36}{7} =$        6] $\dfrac{35}{6} =$

7] $\dfrac{26}{8} =$        8] $\dfrac{7}{2} =$        9] $\dfrac{9}{4} =$

**WRITE THE SIMPLIFIED ANSWERS HERE:**

1. _______________    4. _______________    7. _______________

2. _______________    5. _______________    8. _______________

3. _______________    6. _______________    9. _______________

**SIMPLIFY THE FRACTIONS BELOW. WRITE YOUR ANSWERS IN THE SPACE PROVIDED.**

1] $\dfrac{26}{4} =$

2] $\dfrac{10}{3} =$

3] $\dfrac{51}{8} =$

4] $\dfrac{27}{7} =$

5] $\dfrac{109}{10} =$

6] $\dfrac{22}{3} =$

7] $\dfrac{39}{5} =$

8] $\dfrac{14}{5} =$

9] $\dfrac{9}{2} =$

**WRITE THE SIMPLIFIED ANSWERS HERE:**

1. __________

2. __________

3. __________

4. __________

5. __________

6. __________

7. __________

8. __________

9. __________

## MIXED AND IMPROPER FRACTIONS — ACTIVITY NO: 8

**SIMPLIFY THE FRACTIONS BELOW. WRITE YOUR ANSWERS IN THE SPACE PROVIDED.**

1] $\dfrac{16}{3} =$ 

2] $\dfrac{74}{8} =$ 

3] $\dfrac{17}{3} =$ 

4] $\dfrac{89}{10} =$ 

5] $\dfrac{35}{4} =$ 

6] $\dfrac{61}{6} =$ 

7] $\dfrac{6}{4} =$ 

8] $\dfrac{39}{6} =$ 

9] $\dfrac{107}{10} =$ 

**WRITE THE SIMPLIFIED ANSWERS HERE:**

1. ________

2. ________

3. ________

4. ________

5. ________

6. ________

7. ________

8. ________

9. ________

## SIMPLIFY THE FRACTIONS BELOW. WRITE YOUR ANSWERS IN THE SPACE PROVIDED.

1) $\dfrac{51}{7} =$

2) $\dfrac{22}{8} =$

3) $\dfrac{29}{6} =$

4) $\dfrac{17}{2} =$

5) $\dfrac{5}{4} =$

6) $\dfrac{17}{5} =$

7) $\dfrac{12}{10} =$

8) $\dfrac{21}{4} =$

9) $\dfrac{5}{3} =$

**WRITE THE SIMPLIFIED ANSWERS HERE:**

1. _____________

2. _____________

3. _____________

4. _____________

5. _____________

6. _____________

7. _____________

8. _____________

9. _____________

## SIMPLIFY THE FRACTIONS BELOW. WRITE YOUR ANSWERS IN THE SPACE PROVIDED.

1] $\dfrac{84}{8} =$    2] $\dfrac{64}{7} =$    3] $\dfrac{34}{4} =$

4] $\dfrac{8}{3} =$    5] $\dfrac{38}{8} =$    6] $\dfrac{62}{7} =$

7] $\dfrac{62}{10} =$    8] $\dfrac{28}{6} =$    9] $\dfrac{20}{6} =$

**WRITE THE SIMPLIFIED ANSWERS HERE:**

1. __________    4. __________    7. __________

2. __________    5. __________    8. __________

3. __________    6. __________    9. __________

## SIMPLIFY THE FRACTIONS BELOW. WRITE YOUR ANSWERS IN THE SPACE PROVIDED.

1] $6 \dfrac{2}{6} =$    2] $3 \dfrac{1}{7} =$    3] $1 \dfrac{2}{5} =$

4] $4 \dfrac{1}{8} =$    5] $2 \dfrac{1}{6} =$    6] $10 \dfrac{4}{6} =$

7] $7 \dfrac{4}{6} =$    8] $8 \dfrac{6}{7} =$    9] $3 \dfrac{2}{5} =$

**WRITE THE SIMPLIFIED ANSWERS HERE:**

1. ______________   4. ______________   7. ______________

2. ______________   5. ______________   8. ______________

3. ______________   6. ______________   9. ______________

# SIMPLIFY THE FRACTIONS BELOW. WRITE YOUR ANSWERS IN THE SPACE PROVIDED.

1] $6\dfrac{2}{10} =$

2] $8\dfrac{1}{9} =$

3] $2\dfrac{1}{3} =$

4] $9\dfrac{4}{6} =$

5] $2\dfrac{1}{2} =$

6] $3\dfrac{2}{3} =$

7] $5\dfrac{2}{4} =$

8] $9\dfrac{2}{8} =$

9] $8\dfrac{1}{7} =$

**WRITE THE SIMPLIFIED ANSWERS HERE:**

1. __________

2. __________

3. __________

4. __________

5. __________

6. __________

7. __________

8. __________

9. __________

SIMPLIFY THE FRACTIONS BELOW. WRITE YOUR ANSWERS IN THE SPACE PROVIDED.

1] $5 \dfrac{5}{8} =$

2] $7 \dfrac{6}{7} =$

3] $6 \dfrac{1}{2} =$

4] $6 \dfrac{4}{8} =$

5] $5 \dfrac{4}{6} =$

6] $8 \dfrac{3}{10} =$

7] $1 \dfrac{8}{9} =$

8] $9 \dfrac{8}{9} =$

9] $10 \dfrac{6}{9} =$

WRITE THE SIMPLIFIED ANSWERS HERE:

1. _____________

2. _____________

3. _____________

4. _____________

5. _____________

6. _____________

7. _____________

8. _____________

9. _____________

# SIMPLIFY THE FRACTIONS BELOW. WRITE YOUR ANSWERS IN THE SPACE PROVIDED.

1] $7 \dfrac{1}{4} =$

2] $9 \dfrac{1}{2} =$

3] $10 \dfrac{8}{9} =$

4] $8 \dfrac{4}{6} =$

5] $5 \dfrac{5}{6} =$

6] $1 \dfrac{6}{9} =$

7] $10 \dfrac{5}{9} =$

8] $9 \dfrac{7}{8} =$

9] $2 \dfrac{7}{8} =$

**WRITE THE SIMPLIFIED ANSWERS HERE:**

1. __________

2. __________

3. __________

4. __________

5. __________

6. __________

7. __________

8. __________

9. __________

## SIMPLIFY THE FRACTIONS BELOW. WRITE YOUR ANSWERS IN THE SPACE PROVIDED.

1] $3 \dfrac{3}{5} =$

2] $4 \dfrac{4}{7} =$

3] $2 \dfrac{2}{4} =$

4] $8 \dfrac{6}{10} =$

5] $2 \dfrac{1}{6} =$

6] $2 \dfrac{1}{4} =$

7] $1 \dfrac{1}{3} =$

8] $5 \dfrac{3}{5} =$

9] $7 \dfrac{8}{9} =$

**WRITE THE SIMPLIFIED ANSWERS HERE:**

1. _______________

2. _______________

3. _______________

4. _______________

5. _______________

6. _______________

7. _______________

8. _______________

9. _______________

**SIMPLIFY THE FRACTIONS BELOW. WRITE YOUR ANSWERS IN THE SPACE PROVIDED.**

1] $3 \dfrac{1}{9} =$

2] $7 \dfrac{3}{5} =$

3] $8 \dfrac{2}{6} =$

4] $6 \dfrac{3}{4} =$

5] $10 \dfrac{6}{10} =$

6] $6 \dfrac{4}{8} =$

7] $7 \dfrac{1}{5} =$

8] $1 \dfrac{2}{6} =$

9] $10 \dfrac{8}{9} =$

**WRITE THE SIMPLIFIED ANSWERS HERE:**

1. __________

2. __________

3. __________

4. __________

5. __________

6. __________

7. __________

8. __________

9. __________

## SIMPLIFY THE FRACTIONS BELOW. WRITE YOUR ANSWERS IN THE SPACE PROVIDED.

1] $\dfrac{26}{4} =$

2] $\dfrac{10}{3} =$

3] $\dfrac{51}{8} =$

4] $\dfrac{27}{7} =$

5] $\dfrac{109}{10} =$

6] $\dfrac{22}{3} =$

7] $\dfrac{39}{5} =$

8] $\dfrac{14}{5} =$

9] $\dfrac{9}{2} =$

**WRITE THE SIMPLIFIED ANSWERS HERE:**

1. __________
2. __________
3. __________

4. __________
5. __________
6. __________

7. __________
8. __________
9. __________

## SIMPLIFY THE FRACTIONS BELOW. WRITE YOUR ANSWERS IN THE SPACE PROVIDED.

1] $\dfrac{16}{3} =$

2] $\dfrac{74}{8} =$

3] $\dfrac{17}{3} =$

4] $\dfrac{89}{10} =$

5] $\dfrac{35}{4} =$

6] $\dfrac{61}{6} =$

7] $\dfrac{6}{4} =$

8] $\dfrac{39}{6} =$

9] $\dfrac{107}{10} =$

**WRITE THE SIMPLIFIED ANSWERS HERE:**

1. _______________

2. _______________

3. _______________

4. _______________

5. _______________

6. _______________

7. _______________

8. _______________

9. _______________

GREAT JOB!

# ANSWERS



Shade in the fraction to solve the problem.

1)  +  = 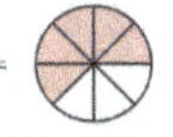

2)  +  = 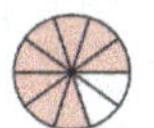

3)  +  = 

4) 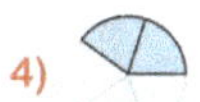 + 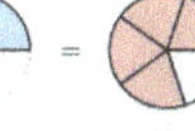 = 

5)  + 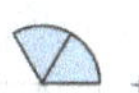 = 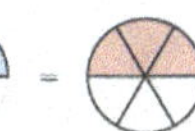

1) $\dfrac{3}{8} + \dfrac{2}{8} = \dfrac{5}{8}$

2) $\dfrac{3}{10} + \dfrac{5}{10} = \dfrac{8}{10}$

3) $\dfrac{2}{8} + \dfrac{1}{8} = \dfrac{3}{8}$

4) $\dfrac{2}{5} + \dfrac{2}{5} = \dfrac{4}{5}$

5) $\dfrac{2}{6} + \dfrac{1}{6} = \dfrac{3}{6}$



Shade in the fraction to solve the problem.

1)  +  = 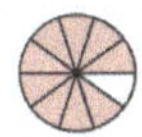

2)  + 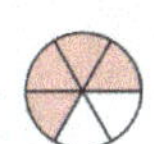 = 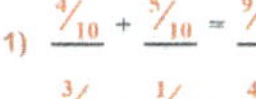

3)  + 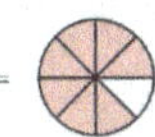 = 

4)  + 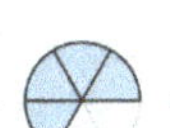 = 

5)  +  =

1) $\dfrac{4}{10} + \dfrac{5}{10} = \dfrac{9}{10}$

2) $\dfrac{3}{6} + \dfrac{1}{6} = \dfrac{4}{6}$

3) $\dfrac{3}{8} + \dfrac{4}{8} = \dfrac{7}{8}$

4) $\dfrac{1}{6} + \dfrac{4}{6} = \dfrac{5}{6}$

5) $\dfrac{4}{12} + \dfrac{1}{12} = \dfrac{5}{12}$

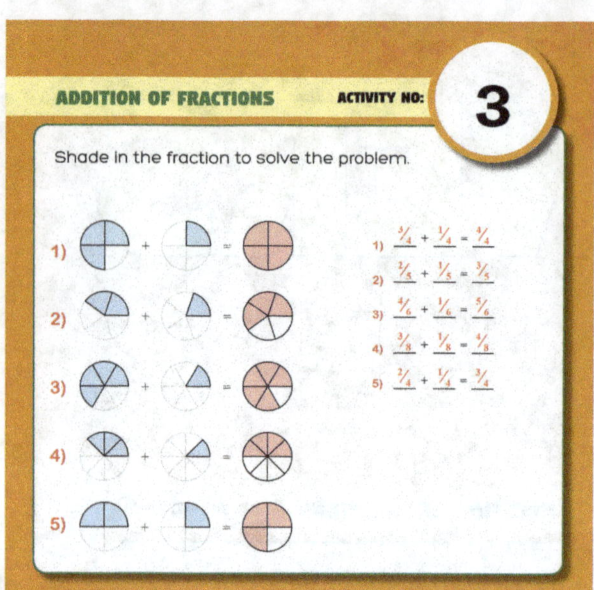


ADDITION OF FRACTIONS
ACTIVITY NO: 3
Shade in the fraction to solve the problem.
1) $\frac{3}{4} + \frac{1}{4} = \frac{4}{4}$
2) $\frac{2}{5} + \frac{1}{5} = \frac{3}{5}$
3) $\frac{4}{6} + \frac{1}{6} = \frac{5}{6}$
4) $\frac{3}{8} + \frac{1}{8} = \frac{4}{8}$
5) $\frac{2}{4} + \frac{1}{4} = \frac{3}{4}$


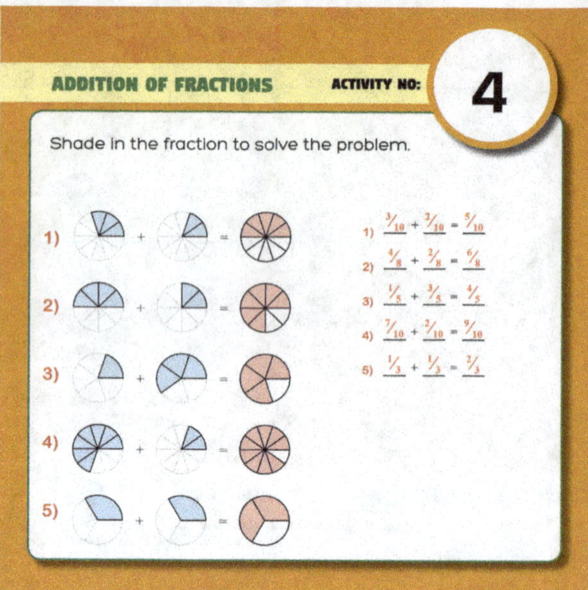


ADDITION OF FRACTIONS
ACTIVITY NO: 4
Shade in the fraction to solve the problem.
1) $\frac{3}{10} + \frac{2}{10} = \frac{5}{10}$
2) $\frac{4}{8} + \frac{2}{8} = \frac{6}{8}$
3) $\frac{1}{5} + \frac{3}{5} = \frac{4}{5}$
4) $\frac{7}{10} + \frac{2}{10} = \frac{9}{10}$
5) $\frac{1}{3} + \frac{1}{3} = \frac{2}{3}$


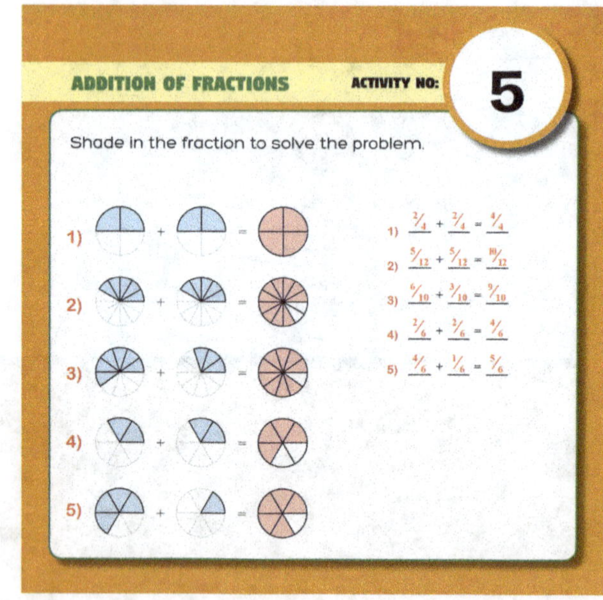


ADDITION OF FRACTIONS
ACTIVITY NO: 5
Shade in the fraction to solve the problem.
1) $\frac{2}{4} + \frac{2}{4} = \frac{4}{4}$
2) $\frac{5}{12} + \frac{5}{12} = \frac{10}{12}$
3) $\frac{6}{10} + \frac{3}{10} = \frac{9}{10}$
4) $\frac{2}{6} + \frac{2}{6} = \frac{4}{6}$
5) $\frac{4}{6} + \frac{1}{6} = \frac{5}{6}$


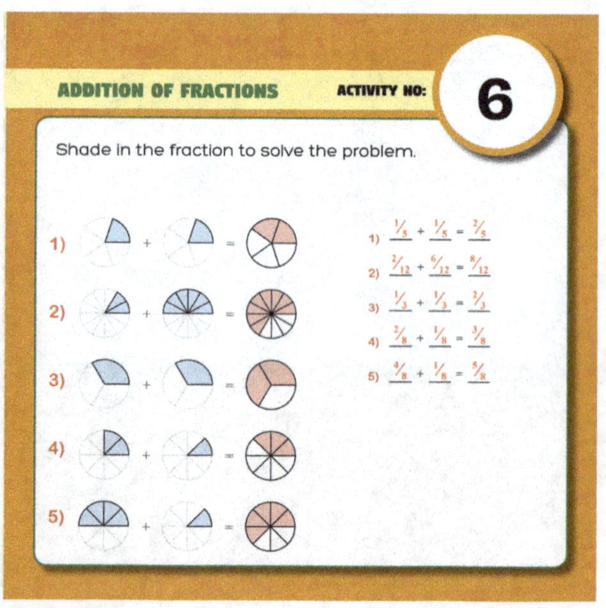


ADDITION OF FRACTIONS
ACTIVITY NO: 6
Shade in the fraction to solve the problem.
1) $\frac{1}{5} + \frac{1}{5} = \frac{2}{5}$
2) $\frac{2}{12} + \frac{6}{12} = \frac{8}{12}$
3) $\frac{1}{3} + \frac{1}{3} = \frac{2}{3}$
4) $\frac{2}{8} + \frac{1}{8} = \frac{3}{8}$
5) $\frac{4}{8} + \frac{1}{8} = \frac{5}{8}$

Shade in the fraction to solve the problem.

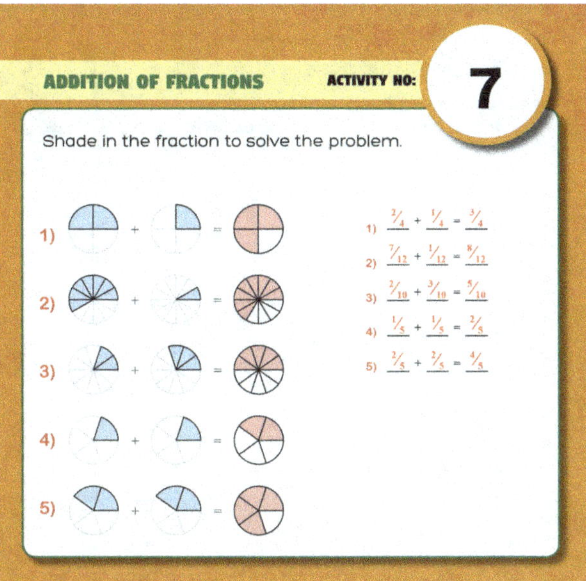

1) $\dfrac{2}{4} + \dfrac{1}{4} = \dfrac{3}{4}$

2) $\dfrac{7}{12} + \dfrac{1}{12} = \dfrac{8}{12}$

3) $\dfrac{2}{10} + \dfrac{3}{10} = \dfrac{5}{10}$

4) $\dfrac{1}{5} + \dfrac{1}{5} = \dfrac{2}{5}$

5) $\dfrac{2}{5} + \dfrac{2}{5} = \dfrac{4}{5}$



Shade in the fraction to solve the problem.

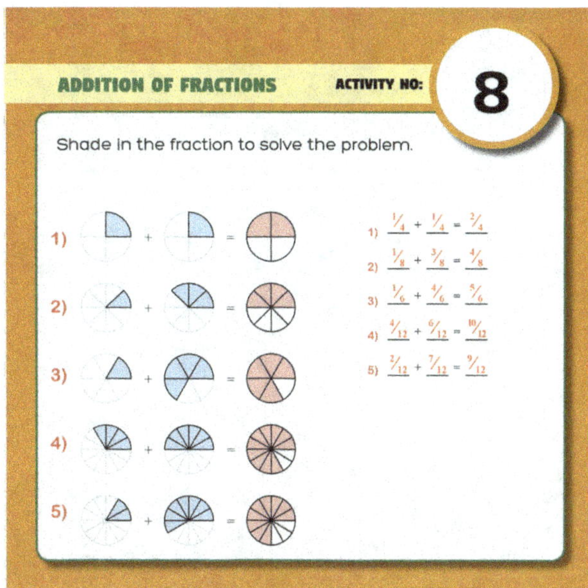

1) $\dfrac{1}{4} + \dfrac{1}{4} = \dfrac{2}{4}$

2) $\dfrac{1}{8} + \dfrac{3}{8} = \dfrac{4}{8}$

3) $\dfrac{1}{6} + \dfrac{4}{6} = \dfrac{5}{6}$

4) $\dfrac{4}{12} + \dfrac{6}{12} = \dfrac{10}{12}$

5) $\dfrac{2}{12} + \dfrac{7}{12} = \dfrac{9}{12}$



Shade in the fraction to solve the problem.

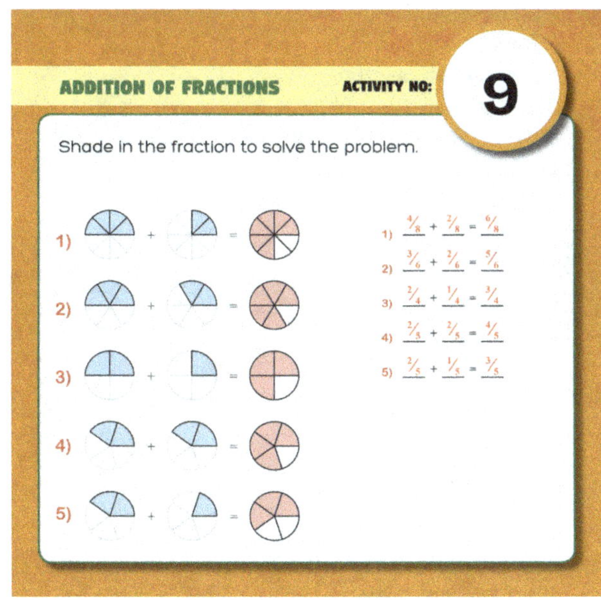

1) $\dfrac{4}{8} + \dfrac{2}{8} = \dfrac{6}{8}$

2) $\dfrac{3}{6} + \dfrac{2}{6} = \dfrac{5}{6}$

3) $\dfrac{2}{4} + \dfrac{1}{4} = \dfrac{3}{4}$

4) $\dfrac{2}{5} + \dfrac{2}{5} = \dfrac{4}{5}$

5) $\dfrac{2}{5} + \dfrac{1}{5} = \dfrac{3}{5}$



Shade in the fraction to solve the problem.

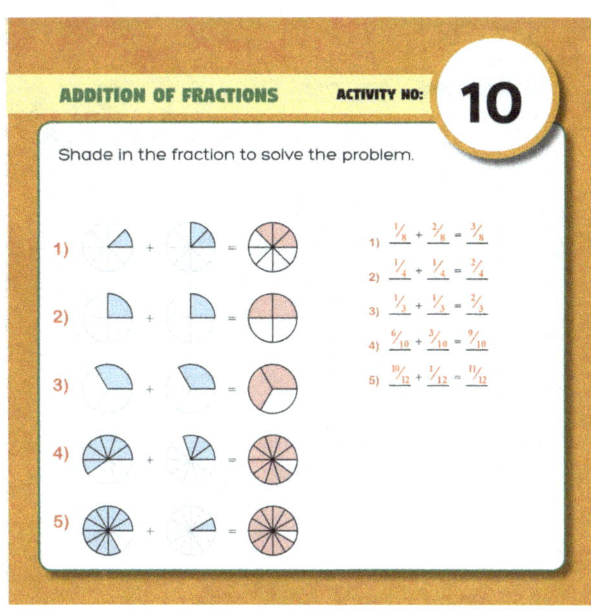

1) $\dfrac{1}{8} + \dfrac{2}{8} = \dfrac{3}{8}$

2) $\dfrac{1}{4} + \dfrac{1}{4} = \dfrac{2}{4}$

3) $\dfrac{1}{3} + \dfrac{1}{3} = \dfrac{2}{3}$

4) $\dfrac{6}{10} + \dfrac{3}{10} = \dfrac{9}{10}$

5) $\dfrac{10}{12} + \dfrac{1}{12} = \dfrac{11}{12}$

SUBTRACTION OF
FRACTIONS
Visual


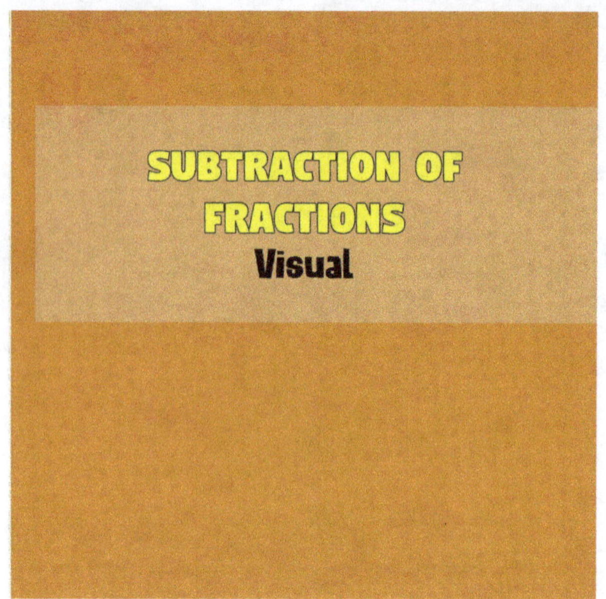

SUBTRACTION OF FRACTIONS        ACTIVITY NO: 1
Shade in the fraction to solve the problem.
Write the simplified answers here:
1.
2.
3.
4.
5.


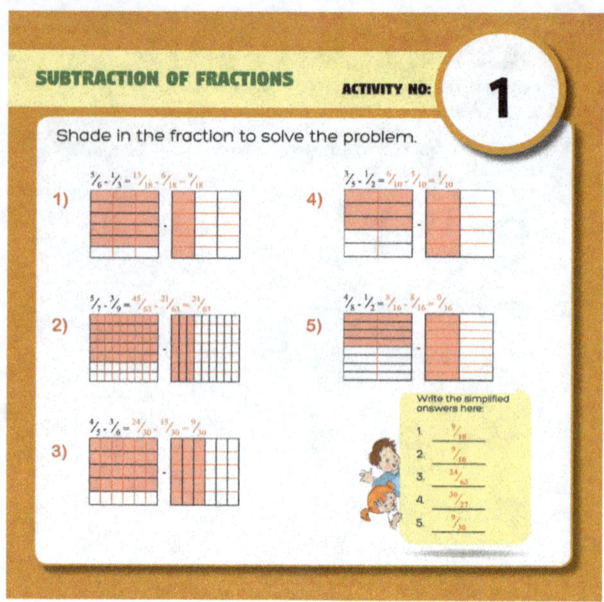

SUBTRACTION OF FRACTIONS        ACTIVITY NO: 2
Shade in the fraction to solve the problem.
Write the simplified answers here:
1.
2.
3.
4.
5.

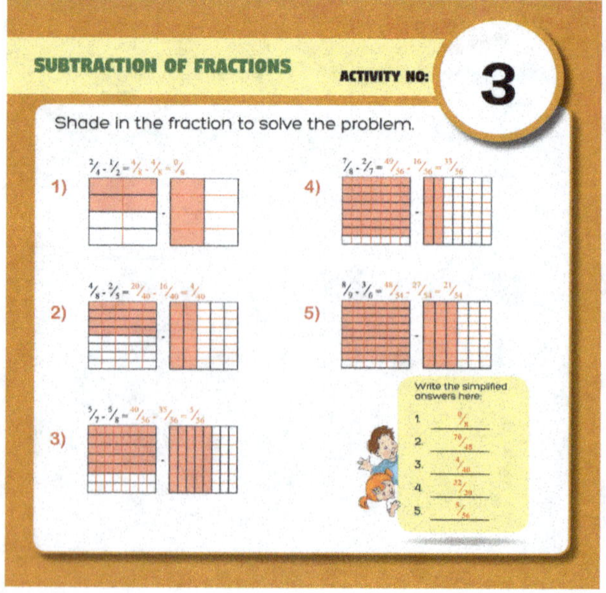

SUBTRACTION OF FRACTIONS        ACTIVITY NO: 3
Shade in the fraction to solve the problem.
Write the simplified answers here:
1.
2.
3.
4.
5.

SUBTRACTION OF FRACTIONS   ACTIVITY NO: 4
Shade in the fraction to solve the problem.
Write the simplified answers here:


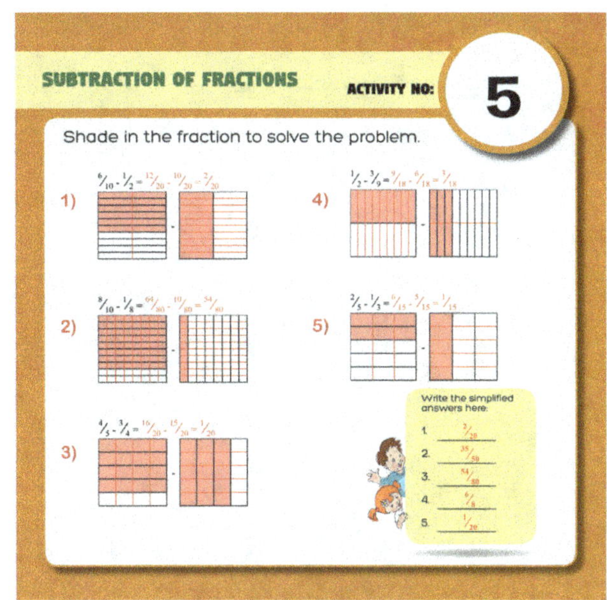


SUBTRACTION OF FRACTIONS   ACTIVITY NO: 5
Shade in the fraction to solve the problem.
Write the simplified answers here:


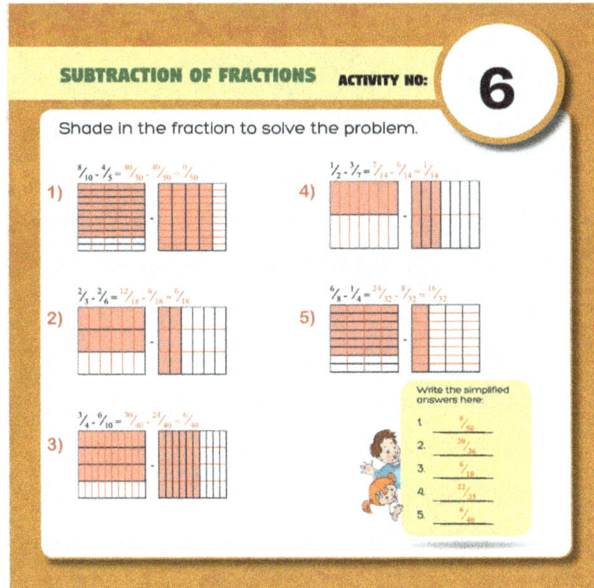


SUBTRACTION OF FRACTIONS   ACTIVITY NO: 6
Shade in the fraction to solve the problem.
Write the simplified answers here:


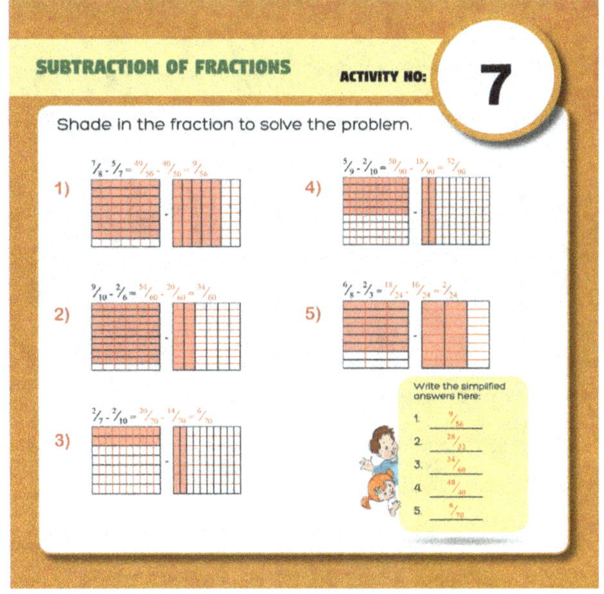


SUBTRACTION OF FRACTIONS   ACTIVITY NO: 7
Shade in the fraction to solve the problem.
Write the simplified answers here:

## SUBTRACTION OF FRACTIONS — ACTIVITY NO: 8

Shade in the fraction to solve the problem.

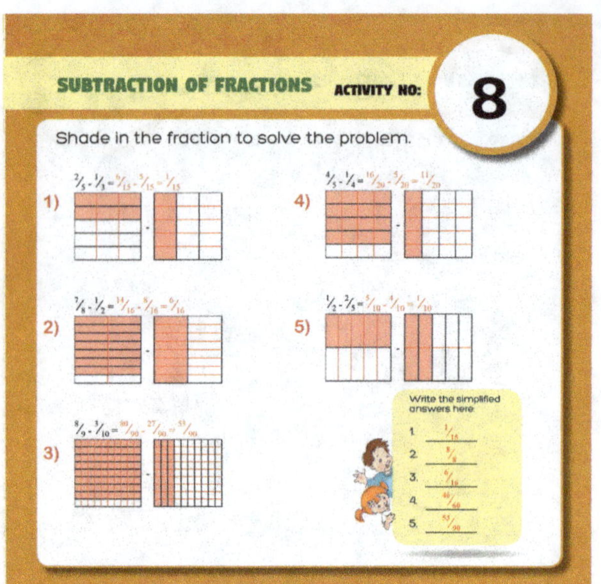



## SUBTRACTION OF FRACTIONS — ACTIVITY NO: 9

Shade in the fraction to solve the problem.

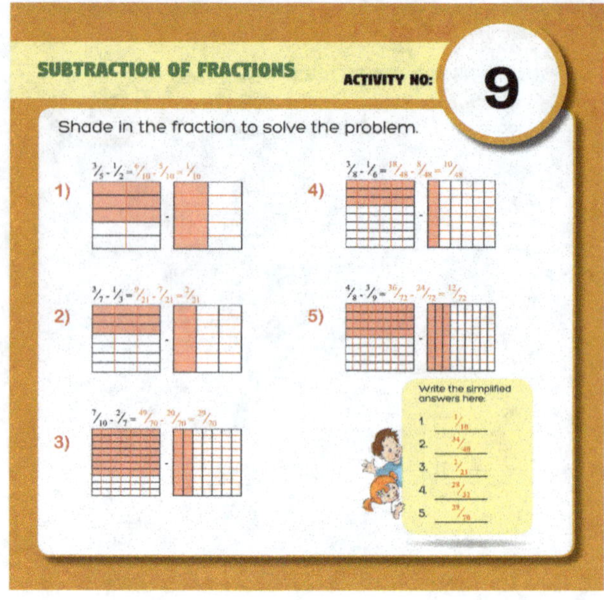



## SUBTRACTION OF FRACTIONS — ACTIVITY NO: 10

Shade in the fraction to solve the problem.

# MIXED AND IMPROPER FRACTIONS

## Convert the improper fraction to amixed number fraction.

$$\frac{17}{5}$$

First divide the numerator by the denominator.

$17 \div 5 = 3\,r2$

$$3\,\frac{2}{5}$$

The 3 is your whole number. While the remainder became the numerator.

$$3\,\frac{2}{5}$$

Your denominator stays the same. And now you have your mixed number.

---



Shade in the fraction to solve the problem.

1] $\dfrac{35}{4} = 8\,\dfrac{3}{4}$    2] $\dfrac{37}{5} = 7\,\dfrac{2}{5}$    3] $\dfrac{13}{7} = 1\,\dfrac{6}{7}$

4] $\dfrac{5}{2} = 2\,\dfrac{1}{2}$    5] $\dfrac{28}{3} = 9\,\dfrac{1}{3}$    6] $\dfrac{25}{3} = 8\,\dfrac{1}{3}$

7] $\dfrac{65}{7} = 9\,\dfrac{2}{7}$    8] $\dfrac{32}{6} = 5\,\dfrac{2}{6}$    9] $\dfrac{36}{5} = 7\,\dfrac{1}{5}$

Write the simplified answers here:

1. $8\,\frac{3}{4}$    4. $2\,\frac{1}{2}$    7. $9\,\frac{2}{7}$
2. $7\,\frac{2}{5}$    5. $9\,\frac{1}{3}$    8. $5\,\frac{2}{6}$
3. $1\,\frac{6}{7}$    6. $8\,\frac{1}{3}$    9. $7\,\frac{1}{5}$

---



Shade in the fraction to solve the problem.

1] $\dfrac{64}{7} = 9\,\dfrac{1}{7}$    2] $\dfrac{12}{7} = 1\,\dfrac{5}{7}$    3] $\dfrac{42}{5} = 8\,\dfrac{2}{5}$

4] $\dfrac{79}{8} = 9\,\dfrac{7}{8}$    5] $\dfrac{66}{7} = 9\,\dfrac{3}{7}$    6] $\dfrac{68}{8} = 8\,\dfrac{4}{8}$

7] $\dfrac{3}{2} = 1\,\dfrac{1}{2}$    8] $\dfrac{19}{3} = 6\,\dfrac{1}{3}$    9] $\dfrac{38}{4} = 9\,\dfrac{2}{4}$

Write the simplified answers here:

1. $9\,\frac{1}{7}$    4. $9\,\frac{7}{8}$    7. $1\,\frac{1}{2}$
2. $1\,\frac{5}{7}$    5. $9\,\frac{3}{7}$    8. $6\,\frac{1}{3}$
3. $8\,\frac{2}{5}$    6. $8\,\frac{4}{8}$    9. $9\,\frac{2}{4}$

---



Shade in the fraction to solve the problem.

1] $\dfrac{32}{5} = 6\,\dfrac{2}{5}$    2] $\dfrac{55}{7} = 7\,\dfrac{6}{7}$    3] $\dfrac{18}{4} = 4\,\dfrac{2}{4}$

4] $\dfrac{13}{2} = 6\,\dfrac{1}{2}$    5] $\dfrac{19}{2} = 9\,\dfrac{1}{2}$    6] $\dfrac{24}{9} = 2\,\dfrac{6}{9}$

7] $\dfrac{55}{6} = 9\,\dfrac{1}{6}$    8] $\dfrac{8}{7} = 1\,\dfrac{1}{7}$    9] $\dfrac{9}{4} = 2\,\dfrac{1}{4}$

Write the simplified answers here:

1. $6\,\frac{2}{5}$    4. $6\,\frac{1}{2}$    7. $9\,\frac{1}{6}$
2. $7\,\frac{6}{7}$    5. $9\,\frac{1}{2}$    8. $1\,\frac{1}{7}$
3. $4\,\frac{2}{4}$    6. $2\,\frac{6}{9}$    9. $2\,\frac{1}{4}$

## MIXED AND IMPROPER FRACTIONS — ACTIVITY NO: 4

Shade in the fraction to solve the problem.

1) $\dfrac{5}{3} = 1\dfrac{2}{3}$  2) $\dfrac{17}{4} = 4\dfrac{1}{4}$  3) $\dfrac{42}{4} = 10\dfrac{2}{4}$

4) $\dfrac{13}{3} = 4\dfrac{1}{3}$  5) $\dfrac{74}{8} = 9\dfrac{2}{8}$  6) $\dfrac{11}{2} = 5\dfrac{1}{2}$

7) $\dfrac{52}{7} = 7\dfrac{3}{7}$  8) $\dfrac{16}{3} = 5\dfrac{1}{3}$  9) $\dfrac{39}{8} = 4\dfrac{7}{8}$

Write the simplified answers here:

1. $1\frac{2}{3}$  4. $4\frac{1}{3}$  7. $7\frac{3}{7}$
2. $4\frac{1}{4}$  5. $9\frac{2}{8}$  8. $5\frac{1}{3}$
3. $10\frac{2}{4}$  6. $5\frac{1}{2}$  9. $4\frac{7}{8}$

## MIXED AND IMPROPER FRACTIONS — ACTIVITY NO: 5

Shade in the fraction to solve the problem.

1) $\dfrac{5}{2} = 2\dfrac{1}{2}$  2) $\dfrac{32}{3} = 10\dfrac{2}{3}$  3) $\dfrac{29}{7} = 4\dfrac{1}{7}$

4) $\dfrac{13}{2} = 6\dfrac{1}{2}$  5) $\dfrac{19}{4} = 4\dfrac{3}{4}$  6) $\dfrac{39}{10} = 3\dfrac{9}{10}$

7) $\dfrac{17}{9} = 1\dfrac{8}{9}$  8) $\dfrac{11}{6} = 1\dfrac{5}{6}$  9) $\dfrac{15}{10} = 1\dfrac{5}{10}$

Write the simplified answers here:

1. $2\frac{1}{2}$  4. $6\frac{1}{2}$  7. $1\frac{8}{9}$
2. $10\frac{2}{3}$  5. $4\frac{3}{4}$  8. $1\frac{5}{6}$
3. $4\frac{1}{7}$  6. $3\frac{9}{10}$  9. $1\frac{5}{10}$

## MIXED AND IMPROPER FRACTIONS — ACTIVITY NO: 6

Shade in the fraction to solve the problem.

1) $\dfrac{39}{7} = 5\dfrac{4}{7}$  2) $\dfrac{9}{2} = 4\dfrac{1}{2}$  3) $\dfrac{31}{3} = 10\dfrac{1}{3}$

4) $\dfrac{29}{5} = 5\dfrac{4}{5}$  5) $\dfrac{36}{7} = 5\dfrac{1}{7}$  6) $\dfrac{35}{6} = 5\dfrac{5}{6}$

7) $\dfrac{26}{8} = 3\dfrac{2}{8}$  8) $\dfrac{7}{2} = 3\dfrac{1}{2}$  9) $\dfrac{9}{4} = 2\dfrac{1}{4}$

Write the simplified answers here:

1. $5\frac{4}{7}$  4. $5\frac{4}{5}$  7. $3\frac{1}{8}$
2. $4\frac{1}{2}$  5. $5\frac{1}{7}$  8. $3\frac{1}{2}$
3. $10\frac{1}{3}$  6. $5\frac{5}{6}$  9. $2\frac{1}{4}$

## MIXED AND IMPROPER FRACTIONS — ACTIVITY NO: 7

Shade in the fraction to solve the problem.

1) $\dfrac{26}{4} = 6\dfrac{2}{4}$  2) $\dfrac{10}{3} = 3\dfrac{1}{3}$  3) $\dfrac{51}{8} = 6\dfrac{3}{8}$

4) $\dfrac{27}{7} = 3\dfrac{6}{7}$  5) $\dfrac{109}{10} = 10\dfrac{9}{10}$  6) $\dfrac{22}{3} = 7\dfrac{1}{3}$

7) $\dfrac{39}{5} = 7\dfrac{4}{5}$  8) $\dfrac{14}{5} = 2\dfrac{4}{5}$  9) $\dfrac{9}{2} = 4\dfrac{1}{2}$

Write the simplified answers here:

1. $6\frac{3}{4}$  4. $3\frac{6}{7}$  7. $7\frac{4}{5}$
2. $3\frac{1}{3}$  5. $10\frac{9}{10}$  8. $2\frac{3}{4}$
3. $6\frac{3}{8}$  6. $7\frac{1}{3}$  9. $4\frac{1}{2}$

## MIXED AND IMPROPER FRACTIONS  ACTIVITY NO: 8

Shade in the fraction to solve the problem.

1) $\dfrac{16}{3} = 5\,\dfrac{1}{3}$   2) $\dfrac{74}{8} = 9\,\dfrac{2}{8}$   3) $\dfrac{17}{3} = 5\,\dfrac{2}{3}$

4) $\dfrac{89}{10} = 8\,\dfrac{9}{10}$   5) $\dfrac{35}{4} = 8\,\dfrac{3}{4}$   6) $\dfrac{61}{6} = 10\,\dfrac{1}{6}$

7) $\dfrac{6}{4} = 1\,\dfrac{2}{4}$   8) $\dfrac{39}{6} = 6\,\dfrac{3}{6}$   9) $\dfrac{107}{10} = 10\,\dfrac{7}{10}$

Write the simplified answers here:

1. $5\,\tfrac{1}{3}$   4. $8\,\tfrac{9}{10}$   7. $1\,\tfrac{2}{4}$
2. $9\,\tfrac{2}{8}$   5. $8\,\tfrac{3}{4}$   8. $6\,\tfrac{3}{6}$
3. $5\,\tfrac{2}{3}$   6. $10\,\tfrac{1}{6}$   9. $10\,\tfrac{7}{10}$

## MIXED AND IMPROPER FRACTIONS  ACTIVITY NO: 9

Shade in the fraction to solve the problem.

1) $\dfrac{51}{7} = 7\,\dfrac{2}{7}$   2) $\dfrac{22}{8} = 2\,\dfrac{6}{8}$   3) $\dfrac{29}{6} = 4\,\dfrac{5}{6}$

4) $\dfrac{17}{2} = 8\,\dfrac{1}{2}$   5) $\dfrac{5}{4} = 1\,\dfrac{1}{4}$   6) $\dfrac{17}{5} = 3\,\dfrac{2}{5}$

7) $\dfrac{12}{10} = 1\,\dfrac{2}{10}$   8) $\dfrac{21}{4} = 5\,\dfrac{1}{4}$   9) $\dfrac{5}{3} = 1\,\dfrac{2}{3}$

Write the simplified answers here:

1. $7\,\tfrac{2}{7}$   4. $8\,\tfrac{1}{2}$   7. $1\,\tfrac{2}{10}$
2. $2\,\tfrac{6}{8}$   5. $1\,\tfrac{1}{4}$   8. $5\,\tfrac{1}{4}$
3. $4\,\tfrac{5}{6}$   6. $3\,\tfrac{2}{5}$   9. $1\,\tfrac{2}{3}$

## MIXED AND IMPROPER FRACTIONS  ACTIVITY NO: 10

Shade in the fraction to solve the problem.

1) $\dfrac{84}{8} = 10\,\dfrac{4}{8}$   2) $\dfrac{64}{7} = 9\,\dfrac{1}{7}$   3) $\dfrac{34}{4} = 8\,\dfrac{2}{4}$

4) $\dfrac{8}{3} = 2\,\dfrac{2}{3}$   5) $\dfrac{38}{8} = 4\,\dfrac{6}{8}$   6) $\dfrac{62}{7} = 8\,\dfrac{6}{7}$

7) $\dfrac{62}{10} = 6\,\dfrac{2}{10}$   8) $\dfrac{28}{6} = 4\,\dfrac{4}{6}$   9) $\dfrac{20}{6} = 3\,\dfrac{2}{6}$

Write the simplified answers here:

1. $10\,\tfrac{4}{8}$   4. $2\,\tfrac{2}{3}$   7. $6\,\tfrac{2}{10}$
2. $9\,\tfrac{1}{7}$   5. $4\,\tfrac{6}{8}$   8. $4\,\tfrac{4}{6}$
3. $8\,\tfrac{2}{4}$   6. $8\,\tfrac{6}{7}$   9. $3\,\tfrac{2}{6}$

## MIXED AND IMPROPER FRACTIONS  ACTIVITY NO: 11

Shade in the fraction to solve the problem.

1) $6\,\dfrac{2}{6} = \dfrac{38}{6}$   2) $3\,\dfrac{1}{7} = \dfrac{22}{7}$   3) $1\,\dfrac{2}{5} = \dfrac{7}{5}$

4) $4\,\dfrac{1}{8} = \dfrac{33}{8}$   5) $2\,\dfrac{1}{6} = \dfrac{13}{6}$   6) $10\,\dfrac{4}{6} = \dfrac{64}{6}$

7) $7\,\dfrac{4}{6} = \dfrac{46}{6}$   8) $8\,\dfrac{6}{7} = \dfrac{62}{7}$   9) $3\,\dfrac{2}{5} = \dfrac{17}{5}$

Write the simplified answers here:

1. $\tfrac{38}{6}$   4. $\tfrac{33}{8}$   7. $\tfrac{46}{6}$
2. $\tfrac{22}{7}$   5. $\tfrac{13}{6}$   8. $\tfrac{62}{7}$
3. $\tfrac{7}{5}$   6. $\tfrac{64}{6}$   9. $\tfrac{17}{5}$

Shade in the fraction to solve the problem.

1] $6\dfrac{2}{10} = \dfrac{62}{10}$    2] $8\dfrac{1}{9} = \dfrac{73}{9}$    3] $2\dfrac{1}{3} = \dfrac{7}{3}$

4] $9\dfrac{4}{6} = \dfrac{58}{6}$    5] $2\dfrac{1}{2} = \dfrac{5}{2}$    6] $3\dfrac{2}{3} = \dfrac{11}{3}$

7] $5\dfrac{2}{4} = \dfrac{22}{4}$    8] $9\dfrac{2}{8} = \dfrac{74}{8}$    9] $8\dfrac{1}{7} = \dfrac{57}{7}$

Write the simplified answers here:

1. $\dfrac{62}{10}$    4. $\dfrac{58}{6}$    7. $\dfrac{22}{4}$

2. $\dfrac{73}{9}$    5. $\dfrac{5}{2}$    8. $\dfrac{74}{8}$

3. $\dfrac{7}{3}$    6. $\dfrac{11}{3}$    9. $\dfrac{57}{7}$




Shade in the fraction to solve the problem.

1] $5\dfrac{5}{8} = \dfrac{45}{8}$    2] $7\dfrac{6}{7} = \dfrac{55}{7}$    3] $6\dfrac{1}{2} = \dfrac{13}{2}$

4] $6\dfrac{4}{8} = \dfrac{52}{8}$    5] $5\dfrac{4}{6} = \dfrac{34}{6}$    6] $8\dfrac{3}{10} = \dfrac{83}{10}$

7] $1\dfrac{8}{9} = \dfrac{17}{9}$    8] $9\dfrac{8}{9} = \dfrac{89}{9}$    9] $10\dfrac{6}{9} = \dfrac{96}{9}$

Write the simplified answers here:

1. $\dfrac{45}{8}$    4. $\dfrac{52}{8}$    7. $\dfrac{17}{9}$

2. $\dfrac{55}{7}$    5. $\dfrac{34}{6}$    8. $\dfrac{89}{9}$

3. $\dfrac{13}{2}$    6. $\dfrac{83}{10}$    9. $\dfrac{96}{9}$




Shade in the fraction to solve the problem.

1] $7\dfrac{1}{4} = \dfrac{29}{4}$    2] $9\dfrac{1}{2} = \dfrac{19}{2}$    3] $10\dfrac{8}{9} = \dfrac{98}{9}$

4] $8\dfrac{4}{6} = \dfrac{52}{6}$    5] $5\dfrac{5}{6} = \dfrac{35}{6}$    6] $1\dfrac{6}{9} = \dfrac{15}{9}$

7] $10\dfrac{5}{9} = \dfrac{95}{9}$    8] $9\dfrac{7}{8} = \dfrac{79}{8}$    9] $2\dfrac{7}{8} = \dfrac{23}{8}$

Write the simplified answers here:

1. $\dfrac{29}{4}$    4. $\dfrac{52}{6}$    7. $\dfrac{95}{9}$

2. $\dfrac{19}{2}$    5. $\dfrac{35}{6}$    8. $\dfrac{79}{8}$

3. $\dfrac{98}{9}$    6. $\dfrac{15}{9}$    9. $\dfrac{23}{8}$




Shade in the fraction to solve the problem.

1] $3\dfrac{3}{5} = \dfrac{18}{5}$    2] $4\dfrac{4}{7} = \dfrac{32}{7}$    3] $2\dfrac{2}{4} = \dfrac{10}{4}$

4] $8\dfrac{6}{10} = \dfrac{86}{10}$    5] $2\dfrac{1}{6} = \dfrac{13}{6}$    6] $2\dfrac{1}{4} = \dfrac{9}{4}$

7] $1\dfrac{1}{3} = \dfrac{4}{3}$    8] $5\dfrac{3}{5} = \dfrac{28}{5}$    9] $7\dfrac{8}{9} = \dfrac{71}{9}$

Write the simplified answers here:

1. $\dfrac{18}{5}$    4. $\dfrac{86}{10}$    7. $\dfrac{4}{3}$

2. $\dfrac{32}{7}$    5. $\dfrac{13}{6}$    8. $\dfrac{28}{5}$

3. $\dfrac{10}{4}$    6. $\dfrac{9}{4}$    9. $\dfrac{71}{9}$

## MIXED AND IMPROPER FRACTIONS — ACTIVITY NO: 16

Shade in the fraction to solve the problem.

1] $3 \frac{1}{9} = \frac{28}{9}$

2] $7 \frac{3}{5} = \frac{38}{5}$

3] $8 \frac{2}{6} = \frac{50}{6}$

4] $6 \frac{3}{4} = \frac{27}{4}$

5] $10 \frac{6}{10} = \frac{106}{10}$

6] $6 \frac{4}{8} = \frac{52}{8}$

7] $7 \frac{1}{5} = \frac{36}{5}$

8] $1 \frac{2}{6} = \frac{8}{6}$

9] $10 \frac{8}{9} = \frac{98}{9}$

Write the simplified answers here:

1. $\frac{28}{9}$
2. $\frac{38}{5}$
3. $\frac{50}{6}$
4. $\frac{27}{4}$
5. $\frac{106}{10}$
6. $\frac{52}{8}$
7. $\frac{36}{5}$
8. $\frac{8}{6}$
9. $\frac{98}{9}$

## MIXED AND IMPROPER FRACTIONS — ACTIVITY NO: 17

Shade in the fraction to solve the problem.

1] $\frac{26}{4} = 6 \frac{2}{4}$

2] $\frac{10}{3} = 3 \frac{1}{3}$

3] $\frac{51}{8} = 6 \frac{3}{8}$

4] $\frac{27}{7} = 3 \frac{6}{7}$

5] $\frac{109}{10} = 10 \frac{9}{10}$

6] $\frac{22}{3} = 7 \frac{1}{3}$

7] $\frac{39}{5} = 7 \frac{4}{5}$

8] $\frac{14}{5} = 2 \frac{4}{5}$

9] $\frac{9}{2} = 4 \frac{1}{2}$

Write the simplified answers here:

1. $6 \frac{2}{4}$
2. $3 \frac{1}{3}$
3. $6 \frac{3}{8}$
4. $3 \frac{6}{7}$
5. $10 \frac{9}{10}$
6. $7 \frac{1}{3}$
7. $7 \frac{4}{5}$
8. $2 \frac{4}{5}$
9. $4 \frac{1}{2}$

## MIXED AND IMPROPER FRACTIONS — ACTIVITY NO: 18

Shade in the fraction to solve the problem.

1] $\frac{16}{3} = 5 \frac{1}{3}$

2] $\frac{74}{8} = 9 \frac{2}{8}$

3] $\frac{17}{3} = 5 \frac{2}{3}$

4] $\frac{89}{10} = 8 \frac{9}{10}$

5] $\frac{35}{4} = 8 \frac{3}{4}$

6] $\frac{61}{6} = 10 \frac{1}{6}$

7] $\frac{6}{4} = 1 \frac{2}{4}$

8] $\frac{39}{6} = 6 \frac{3}{6}$

9] $\frac{107}{10} = 10 \frac{7}{10}$

Write the simplified answers here:

1. $5 \frac{1}{3}$
2. $9 \frac{2}{8}$
3. $5 \frac{2}{3}$
4. $8 \frac{9}{10}$
5. $8 \frac{3}{4}$
6. $10 \frac{1}{6}$
7. $1 \frac{2}{4}$
8. $6 \frac{3}{6}$
9. $10 \frac{7}{10}$

Visit
BABY PROFESSOR
EDUCATION KIDS
www.BabyProfessorBooks.com
to download Free Baby Professor eBooks
and view our catalog of new and exciting
Children's Books